Blood, Guts, and Grease

AMERICAN WARRIORS

Throughout the nation's history, numerous men and women of all ranks and branches of the U.S. military have served their country with honor and distinction. During times of war and peace, there are individuals whose exemplary achievements embody the highest standards of the U.S. armed forces. The aim of the American Warriors series is to examine the unique historical contributions of these individuals, whose legacies serve as enduring examples for soldiers and citizens alike. The series will promote a deeper and more comprehensive understanding of the U.S. armed forces.

SERIES EDITOR: Joseph Craig

An AUSA Book

Blood, Guts, and Grease

George S. Patton in World War I

Jon B. Mikolashek

Foreword by Paul T. Mikolashek

UNIVERSITY PRESS OF KENTUCKY

Scholarly publisher for the Commonwealth,
serving Bellarmine University, Berea College, Centre
College of Kentucky, Eastern Kentucky University,
The Filson Historical Society, Georgetown College,
Kentucky Historical Society, Kentucky State University,
Morehead State University, Murray State University,
Northern Kentucky University, Transylvania University,
University of Kentucky, University of Louisville,
and Western Kentucky University.
All rights reserved.

Editorial and Sales Offices: The University Press of Kentucky
663 South Limestone Street, Lexington, Kentucky 40508-4008
www.kentuckypress.com

Library of Congress Cataloging-in-Publication Data

Names: Mikolashek, Jon, author. | Mikolashek, Paul T. (P.T.), writer of
   foreword.
Title: Blood, guts, and grease : George S. Patton in World War I / Jon B.
   Mikolashek ; foreword by Paul T. Mikolashek.
Description: Lexington, Kentucky : University Press of Kentucky, [2019] |
   Series: American warriors | Includes bibliographical references and index.
Identifiers: LCCN 2019014996| ISBN 9780813177908 (hardcover : alk. paper) |
   ISBN 9780813177922 (pdf) | ISBN 9780813177939 (epub)
Subjects: LCSH: Patton, George S. (George Smith), 1885-1945. | United States.
   Army—Biography. | Generals—United States—Biography. | World War,
   1914–1918—Campaigns. | World War, 1914–1918—Tank warfare. | United
   States. Army. Tank Corps.
Classification: LCC E745.P3 M54 2019 | DDC 355.0092 [B]—dc23

For Melissa and Liz

Contents

Photographs follow page 77.

Foreword

On 16 December 1944 the German Wehrmacht launched three armies in a powerful counteroffensive stunning the Allied Forces in Europe. The German attack began a penetration deep into Allied lines, sending the American forces into confusion and uncertainty. Three days later General Dwight D. Eisenhower met with his key commanders: General Omar Bradley, Air Marshal Sir Arthur Tedder, Lieutenant General Jacob Devers, Eisenhower's chief of staff Lieutenant General Walter Bedell Smith, and Lieutenant General George S. Patton. The situation was grim. The United States–led command had finally come to the realization that this was a dangerous and serious attempt to disrupt the Allied offensive into Germany.

Fortunately, determined defense of the shoulders of the penetration and reinforcements to the key transportation hubs at St. Vith and Bastogne slowed the German efforts, but what was needed was a significant counterattack into the flank of the "Bulge." Enter George S. Patton Jr. When asked if he could counterattack, he responded with "I can attack with three divisions in two days, six divisions in three more days." He was met with disbelief; some thought it just bluff, and Eisenhower told him not to be "fatuous." Patton was not posturing, bluffing, or self-aggrandizing.

Patton had prearranged plans to move his Third US Army 90 degrees while still engaged with an enemy to his front. This was to be done in the middle of a harsh European winter with icy roads and difficult lines of communication.

The situation called for a bold, audacious response, and that is what Patton offered. The plan that followed was not only bold and audacious but an enduring lesson in operational and tactical maneuver and aggressive leadership from the top. It was not a spur-of-the-moment reaction but the product of situational understanding, rapid assessments, and solid staff work and teamwork. Logistically the challenge would seem insurmountable. The outcome was the finest example of maneuver of any field army in United States history. It was all Patton's leadership over the previous years that developed the team, the skills, and the will to execute this maneuver.

The attributes that Patton demonstrated in December 1944 began to develop early in his career with experiences in Mexico and more prominently in World War I. This book takes the reader through those early days of Patton's military life, when he learned to lead from an incredible array of mentors, including John J. Pershing but also less well-known officers like Sam Rockenbach. A student of history, Patton had a grasp of the art of warfare. He was given the opportunity to command the first tank organization in the United States Army—indeed, not only command but organize, train, and equip the first tank brigade and then lead it into combat.

While the focus of this book is clearly on Patton's development as a leader during the First World War, it offers insights into Patton's personal life as well. Patton is larger than life, but also very human with the flaws, interests, and passions that would characterize his future.

Paul T. Mikolashek
Lieutenant General, US Army (Ret)
Commanding General Third US Army, 2000–2002

Introduction

> Patton, we want to start a Tank School, to get anything out of
> tanks one must be reckless and take risks, I think you are the
> sort of darned fool who will do it.
> —quoted in Blumenson, *The Patton Papers*

In 1916, little-known First Lieutenant George S. Patton Jr. was worried
about his career. He believed that only commanding in combat would
allow him to rise through the ranks of the United States Army. Ever since
he was a small child, Patton had dreamt of war and the laurels of victory.
In 1916, World War I was raging in Europe, but for the United States and
Patton there seemed no avenue to join the fight. In less than two years,
however, Patton's life and career would change radically. In twenty-four
months he would rise to the rank of colonel and command a tank brigade
in combat and would earn the Distinguished Service Cross for his bravery
during the start of the Meuse-Argonne campaign. By the end of the war,
Patton would have achieved more than he ever hoped, and it was this
experience that pushed him to even higher command and glory in World
War II. Without his experience in the Great War, the life and history of
George S. Patton could have been remarkably different.

Patton's experience in World War I had significant impact on his
future exploits in the Mediterranean and Europe during World War II.
Yet while numerous studies have been done on Patton in regard to his
personality and command style, next to nothing has been done on what
he did in World War I. The best two biographies of Patton are still Martin Blumenson's *Patton: The Man Behind the Legend*, published in 1985
on the centennial of Patton's birth, and Carlo D'Este's *Patton: A Genius
for War*. D'Este's 1995 work is the most complete and best study on Patton and his entire life. As in other numerous works on Patton's life and
career, his World War I experience is mainly glanced over or ignored altogether. D'Este spends fewer than one hundred pages on the war and Blumenson even fewer. There is no major work on Patton and his experience
in World War I. Dale Wilson wrote an excellent study on the creation of

the Tank Corps titled *Treat 'em Rough: The Birth of American Armor, 1917–1920*, which heaps praise on Patton and his role in the creation of the Tank Corps. Wilson's study remains the standard in the field on the birth of the United States Tank Corps and its performance in World War I, but his emphasis is not on Patton and his command solely. Blumenson, the most renowned Patton historian and editor of the highly acclaimed *Patton Papers*, was one of the great World War II historians and himself a combat historian in that war.[1] Blumenson worked closely with the Patton family, especially Patton's wife Beatrice Patton, on collecting the documents that make up the two volumes based on Patton's diaries.

All three authors are kind to Patton and think highly of his performance in both world wars. Far more critical of Patton is Stanley Hirshson's *General Patton: A Soldier's Life*, published in 2002. Hirshson pays very little attention to Patton's exploits in World War I and overly focuses on some of the more controversial periods of Patton's life. The study is typical of historians when dealing with military figures. Far too often, such historians like to play armchair general and condemn past commanders for mistakes that are clear only through hindsight, time, and the release of historical documents and intelligence reports long after the battle or war is over. This is not to say historians cannot be critical of past historical figures—that would be dereliction of duty—however, historians dealing not only with Patton but with other famous military leaders need to pay better attention to the intelligence then available and to the time pressure the commanders were under when they made, often, life-or-death decisions. The "fog of war" makes military decision-making a tough business for even the greatest commanders, such as Genghis Khan or Napoleon. Most military commanders must rely on years of training, patchy intelligence reports, and luck.

All these works discuss World War I and Patton's role, but for their authors the Great War is clearly secondary to World War II. The same goes for the public. Every year works are produced on Patton, and every year Americans are more than willing to read and consume them; however, like professional historians, the public knows very little about his World War I experience.

For many years, then, publishers and audiences only wanted to focus on his World War II exploits. The movie *Patton*, while great, has shaped how the public views Patton. The movie begins and ends in World War II. It makes the audience believe that Patton emerged from nothing into command and success. It appears that General Patton was and always had been as portrayed so brilliantly by George C. Scott. But Patton was not an overnight success. He spent decades in the army before garnering national attention in World War II. Studies done on military leaders tend to deal almost exclusively with their ultimate successes, such as Patton's leadership during the invasion of North Africa or the Battle of the Bulge. While these events are particularly important, most historians neglect the fact that the officers learned much of the art of command and the science of control in previous battles, experiences, and wars, not just in the classroom or through the progression of rank throughout their career. Prior to World War II, Patton's best training ground was not in a garrison army or at Fort Leavenworth's staff college, but instead on the fields of France in World War I.

With the events and publications marking the centennial of the Great War, Americans have started to pay more attention to World War I and the small but important role the United States played in the conflict. Compared to nations like France and Germany, the United States' role was rather limited. Patton participated in only two campaigns or major operations, the reduction of the St. Mihiel salient and the Meuse-Argonne campaign. His tank brigade, with a few thousand soldiers and a couple hundred tanks, helped the Allies bring the war to a victorious end in November 1918. For Patton, the war taught many lessons. First, he went into combat and confirmed that he could lead men in battle. Second, he understood he could command larger units and, with more experience and training, increasingly large units in the United States Army. Third, the Great War reinforced his views on discipline, correctness, and cleanliness, which would be reflected in his command and leadership style in World War II. Fourth, and arguably the most important way the war was beneficial to Patton, it exposed him to one of the greatest innovations in warfare, the tank. Patton was the first and remains the greatest tanker in American military history. It was in World War I that he learned about the tank, tank tactics, and modern warfare, and the war made him reflect and think deeply during the interwar period about the future of war. Patton, along with his good friend Dwight D. Eisenhower and other officers, realized tanks were the future of ground combat and would play a larger role in the next war. Without this experience, Patton might not have been prepared for World War II and, given his age, could have been lost not only to the army but to history.

Without experience in World War I, Patton would never have learned his up-front and aggressive leadership as, for the first time in his life, he led men into battle. Also, Patton has always been associated with the tank, which in 1918 was a crude armored behemoth. As the first tanker in the United States Army, Patton laid the groundwork for his future triumphs in World War II, and for the armored forces in the United States. Without his experience in World War I, Patton might never have learned the art of command, or how to lead soldiers and tanks. Without this experience Patton might have become what he most feared: nothing.

Before Patton's career was made, he would deploy unexpectedly to Mexico with General John J. Pershing and would lead the first motorized attack in United States Army history. It was in Mexico that Patton first garnered minor national attention and saw how motorized vehicles could be used to fight and win wars.

As early as 1914, Patton was concerned about his reputation and his chance to make an impact. While only in his late twenties, he wrote to his father, George S. Patton Sr., about the war in Europe: "If the war is to be short there will be no chance for a man of my rank to make any reputation as a leader of men but it might afford an opportunity to make a personal record on which to be something in the future. Such a personal reputation can be gotten better with regulars than with the malatia [sic]."[2]

Patton later in the letter contemplated leaving the regular army and joining a state militia, solely to gain greater rank. Patton wrote that if the wars in both Europe and Mexico were to drag on, it might be a good career move to resign his active commission and get into a fight and earn a reputation as a warrior. "Hence should I succeed in becoming notorious you must try to get me a place as a major at least of state cavalry as I think infantry will not have so good a chance in Mexico as mounted troops."[3] Patton entertained the idea for a few months, and gave it serious thought; however, his mind was likely made up for him when then-Major Hugh A. Drum, who would rise to fame in World War I and would remain one of Patton's great mentors, told him: "Don't think of attempting anything of the kind, at present. If you can get a leave, all right; but go to look on. We don't want to waste youngsters of your sort in the service of foreign nations unless they need you more than appears to be the case now."[4] Drum offered good advice, and Patton dropped the idea of leaving the regular army. Patton realized that the war in Europe was going to last for some time and that eventually the United States would be drawn into the conflict. He would wait and, through hard work and luck, would move rapidly up the ranks in four short years. Patton, perhaps more than his fellow officers, sought out senior officers for mentorship and career advancement. Then as now, mentorship was something many junior officers would actively seek out. Often, however, an organic relationship would emerge over time and when personalities worked well together. Patton, who was prone to anger and bombastic language, seldom liked his senior leaders, but Drum was one of the few, along with John J. Pershing, that he respected and trusted.

As the war in Europe entered its second year, Patton began to grow impatient and lashed out against United States foreign policy decisions and the presidency of Woodrow Wilson, whom he despised both personally and politically. Patton, as he would do in World War I and throughout his life, vented often to his father in long-winded and colorful letters. Much more a saber rattler than his father, George S. Patton Jr., would have preferred to enter the war in 1914, and especially after the sinking of the *Lusitania* in 1915, he admonished his father for not pushing for war:

Another view of the case which is very pertinent and hence not mentioned in any of our fool papers, is the fact that the Lusitania carried $2000000.00 dollars worth of cartridges. Each cartridge costs 3 cents so you get 6 666666.66 cartridges which at a liberal estimate would wound 6 666 german soldiers who are certainly worth more than 1000 civilians many of whom would have died any way from the diseases of child hood. . . . For as I think that we ought to declare war if Germany failes [*sic*] as she should to pay heed to our foolish talk.[5]

Patton ended the letter by arguing over law and the military and told his father, "There is one International Law—the best Army."[6]

Often Patton's letters to his father and other family members would end on a lighter note, possibly to deflect his father's anger. While father and son always maintained a close relationship, the two disagreed often on politics and diplomacy, and apparently on the legal system! Patton's father was a lawyer and became a politician of some renown in California. Patton never understood how his father could support a president like Woodrow Wilson, writing in July 1916: "I would like to go to hell so that I might be able to shovel a few extra coals on that unspeakable ass Wilson how you can support him is beyond me and if he is reelected the American *People* are worse than even I imagine."[7] George S. Patton Sr., unlike his son, was naturally easygoing and politically savvy. He was often a calming influence on his son's life, and though his son may not have heeded all his advice, it was clear George Jr. respected and revered his father.

There was just one other man whom Patton respected and revered in equal measure. That man was General John J. Pershing. Prior to Pershing's expedition into Mexico in 1916, Patton was only a lieutenant and, like other officers of his age and rank, had no hope for promotion anytime soon. The United States Army of the early twentieth century was little different from the United States Army that massively grew during the American Civil War and then rapidly demobilized. Promotions were much slower than in today's army. Currently it takes a little over three years for a newly commissioned officer to make captain. Patton had been in the army nearly ten years and was still a first lieutenant. Officers of Patton's era could serve thirty years or more and not make major.[8] However, his promotion rate was about to increase rapidly as the threat of war increased, and Patton had major advantages over nearly every officer in the United States Army. Due to her vast family fortune, the woman he married, Beatrice Ayer, had numerous political connections. And a growing relationship between Patton's sister, Nita, and General Pershing allowed Patton to become an aide to Pershing as the United States Army readied for active service in Mexico. Pershing would become the role model whom Patton would emulate for the remainder of his life. Born on 13 September 1860, Pershing graduated from West Point in 1886, and while not a great student, he was president of his class and earned the respect of teachers and fellow students. Like most officers in the army during this time, he first managed to achieve rank by waiting his turn and being in the right place at the right time.[9] Along the way Pershing was nicknamed Black Jack, an insulting reference he loathed, due to his having once commanded the 10th Cavalry Regiment, a black unit in the United States Army.[10] After Pancho Villa and his band of rebels attacked Columbus, New Mexico, on 9 March 1916, Pershing was selected to command the American Punitive Expedition into Mexico and performed well enough that, following the United States' declaration of war against Germany, he was selected to command the American Expeditionary Force.

As a soldier and commander, Pershing was everything Patton wanted to be. Strong jawed, muscular, and imposing, Pershing garnered respect just by walking into the room. A tough disciplinarian, Pershing demanded the most from his staff and soldiers, and his aides lived in fear of his wrath. Many a good soldier lost his career by failing Pershing. Throughout the Mexican campaign and the brief time as his aide in Europe, Patton began to emulate Pershing. While Patton was already known as a loudmouthed martinet, it was during his time under Pershing that he refined his ideas and beliefs on military protocol. Among his troops in the Tank Corps, his form of discipline became notorious, and this helped the legend of Patton grow. Later in Europe, Patton introduced himself to his new soldiers with an expletive-laden talk that would become more famous in World War II: "Why, you goddamned sons of bitches, do you think the Marines are tough? Well, you just wait until I get through with you. Being tough will save lives."[11] He was so strict about salutes, a perfect salute became known a Georgie Patton.

More than his habits on discipline, Patton learned what it took to be a commander. For the first time he learned the art of leading many men into battle. From serving under Pershing, Patton grew as a person and as a military officer and leader. Without Pershing's influence, Patton would have been a much different man. Certainly, without Pershing's political influence, Patton would never have risen in rank so quickly or enjoyed his future military achievements. Over the years their friendship grew, and while Pershing broke off his engagement to Nita Patton, the two men loved one another, Pershing being the father and Patton the wide-eyed obedient son. Prior to leaving for North Africa in 1942, the last thing Patton did was pay his respects to a dying Pershing at Walter Reed Hospital. Unfortunately, following Patton's slapping of two sick soldiers in a medical tent in Sicily, Pershing was so disgusted with him that they never spoke again, and Pershing ultimately outlived Patton. Regardless, Pershing's influence on Patton was immense, and without it Patton most likely would never have achieved his fame and success.

The Punitive Expedition on which the United States Army was sent into Mexico (now called simply the Mexican Expedition) began in mid-March 1916, more than a year before Patton and the United States could enter the war in Europe. The expedition would play an important role in Patton's life and career as he used his sister Nita's relationship with General Pershing to get a position on the staff of the future chief of the American Expeditionary Force in France. The breezy and beautiful Nita was seeing Pershing all during this time and right up until Pershing left for Europe in 1917. The two got along immediately, even though Patton's father did not approve of the match. George Sr. found Pershing too rigid and believed Nita could do much better. As for her brother, while George Jr. used Nita's growing relationship with Pershing to advance his career, he was rather ambivalent about it. He did not like the taint of favoritism, and when their engagement crumbled during World War I, he was almost relieved, for it meant he would have to make it all by himself, and if he did, it would be based on his own personal merit. Pershing would

remain a widower and later in life would regret the decision not to marry
Nita. As Carlo D'Este wrote after the war, Pershing after a night of drinking told Patton, "Georgie, Georgie, if I hadn't been such a damn egotistic
fool, my children would have been just a little younger than your children with the same beautiful blond hair, and the same true blue eyes."[12]

By the spring of 1916, Patton wrote to his father about the operation in Mexico, "They can't beat us but they will kill a lot of us. Not me
though."[13] Patton was anxious to get into a fight, but he was convinced
he would make it out just fine. It is not uncommon for soldiers and officers to think this way. Patton hoped the war with Mexico would last a
little while so he could gain rank and a reputation, telling his father, "If
it turns out to be a long war there ought to be volunteer regiments later
so if I do well keep an eye out and get me a job. As I told you when you
were here I think it would be a mistake to enter the Vol. at first but if
one had a reputation in the regulars a high commission could be gotten
later."[14] Patton went so far as to write to Captain R. F. McReynolds of
the California militia asking for a commission as a major.[15] As he would
show throughout his career, Patton was always pushing for higher rank
and more authority, but not because of a pay raise, as his wife, Beatrice,
was wealthy enough to make him one of the richest officers in the army.
It was, instead, because he wanted to attain supreme rank and play an
important role in military history. In the same letter to his father, Patton
showed his devilish side, writing that "there should be a law killing fat
colonels on sight."[16] However, before he would push for a high rank in
the state militia, fate and Patton's aggressive nature would make the decision to leave active duty a moot point. One of the most important days
in Patton's life was about to play out and, for the first time in his career,
give him a taste of combat, as well as public acclaim. On 14 May 1916,
Patton got what he had long pursued: he found a way into a fight.

Patton wrote a detailed and glowing letter of the affair to his father
the next day:

At last I succeeded in getting into a fight. I went out yesterday to
buy corn and as I got near to San Miguel where I had been before
hunting for Julio Cardenes I decided to combine business with
pleasure and see if I could get him[.] the slope of the ground con-
cealed me from view until I was about a mile and a half from the
house[.] when I topped the ridge I speeded up as fast as I could
and went past the house when I jumped out and halted the other
two cars at the other corner and had men run around that end.

Then I ran for the front door followed by Mr. Lunt a guide who was unarmed[.] when I got about 20 yards from the gate three armed Mex. [r]ode out[.] as I thought they might be Carranza men I did not shout[.] they started around the end away from me when they met my men and turned back all firing at me at about 20 yards or less[.] I fired back five times with my new pistol and one of them ducked back into the house. I found later that this was Cardenes and that I had hit both he and his horse.[17]

Julio Cárdenas (whose name Patton had, typically, misspelled) was one of Pancho Villa's chief lieutenants, and by luck Patton had managed to find him in a compromised position: "Soon I saw the private shooting he fired twice and shook his head then he fired a third time look back and grinned at me holding up one finger. That was Cardenes who arm I had broken and after he went out the back window he was shot twice in the right lung but still ran about five hundred yards and shot 30 times."[18]

While this event would likely be little more than a footnote to history had Patton not gone on to fame in World War II, it is an important piece of American military history, and too little remembered. As Patton would recount for the rest of his life, his action here was indeed the first time a motorized vehicle was used in an attack on an enemy. Patton was correct, although this was a relatively minor skirmish and not an epic battle on the scale of what was happening across the Atlantic. Patton would later use the shooting of Cárdenas to land his position in the Tank Corps, and in another letter to his father written overseas in 1917, he suggested as much: "I have a hunch that my Mexican Auto Battle was the fore runner of this who can say?"[19] There is little doubt his firefight in April 1916 helped Patton's career, but the influence of the "battle" was embellished over the last hundred years, and largely by Patton himself. No doctrinal changes occurred because of Patton's aggressive attack in Mexico, but it boosted his career and gave him some national acclaim as newspapers picked up on the story. Although the United States Army did not change how they operated or trained based on Patton's motorized attack, it was the first, and that alone makes it of historical importance. More important for Patton, he likely endeared himself more to Pershing, as following the attack he "tied the corpses on the hoods of the cars[.] were just starting when we saw about forty men galliping towards us[.] we withdrew gracefully. As no one knew where we were and our gas tanks were in read made me hesitate to fight them."[20] Patton personally delivered the Mexican second-in-command's corpse to Pershing, who then referred to

Patton as "The Bandit."[21] Pershing allowed Patton to keep Cárdenas's saddle and saber as war trophies. Patton's life and career would have been dramatically altered if his automobile did not start or he ran out of gas, but personally Patton achieved minor notoriety out of the fight, and he impressed himself with his performance under fire, as he wrote: "I was much less scared than I had thought I would be, in fact all that worried me was the fear they would get away."[22] Later Patton, who wrote nearly daily to his wife Beatrice, told her, "You are probably wondering if my conscience hurts me for killing a man[.] it does not. I feel about it just as I did when I got my sword fish, surprised at my luck."[23] This minor engagement finally proved to Patton that he could fight and maintain his coolness. This coolness would be tested in major combat sooner than he realized.

On 2 April 1917, President Wilson gave a roaring speech to Congress, and Congress responded by officially declaring war on the German and Austrian Empires. For Patton and the United States military, it was time to organize, expand, and arrive in Europe en masse as soon as possible. Patton's father, ever the Wilson supporter, who hated war, wrote a loving letter to his son:

> As to sending a force to Europe it seems on its face a foolish thing to do—but it may never the less be forced by T.R. and the press. It does seem absurd, that men like Pershing & others should in such event be passed over and the glory given to such a "soldier" as T.R. . . . I hate to think of you going—but I would hate you to be passed over if you want to go. . . . If I were younger I would wish above all things to go—first because of duty—but also to enjoy the thrill of fighting the German menace to civilization.[24]

For George S. Patton Jr., the war was a godsend to his career, but first he had to get an overseas assignment. Unlike most officers, including fellow officer Dwight D. Eisenhower, Patton would use his growing relationship with Pershing to gain a position on his staff and would be one of the first American officers overseas.

1

Off to Paris
Here Come the Americans
(28 May–15 December 1917)

> I am a sort of "Pooh-Bah" and do everything no one else does.
> —Patton to Beatrice Patton, 29 July 1917

On 6 April 1917, President Woodrow Wilson and the United States declared war on Germany. Some, like former president Theodore Roosevelt, were relieved that finally the United States could help out its allies and make a mark on international affairs. Others, like George Patton Sr., thought the declaration was a terrible idea and that America had no business in European affairs.

For the United States, war was now certain, but the question had to be asked, what would the United States fight with? In 1917 the United States' regular army was equivalent to those of such nations as Chile, Denmark, and even the Netherlands.[1] More specifically, the United States Army had around 285,000 Springfield rifles, 544 three-inch field guns, and only enough ammunition for a nine-hour bombardment. Also, at a time when airplanes were new and fairly primitive, the United States had fifty-five planes, and of this number 93 percent were obsolete.[2] To make matters worse, some divisions, now filled with raw recruits in training, had to first chisel their weapons out of wood before practicing with them. In more extreme cases, some recruits got to Europe without ever seeing a rifle. Still, the United States' declaration of war gave France and Great Britain hope that the Great War could end soon, and it sent shivers down the backs of the Kaiser and the German High Command.

What the United States Army lacked in supplies, it surely made up in men. What the English and French governments wanted most was men to fill their weakening lines. In order to build its army and fight the war, the United States instituted the Selective Service System to draft men from the age of 18 to 35 (later raised to 45). By the end of the war, 24 million

Americans had registered and 2.75 million were drafted.[3] With a declaration of war in hand, and supplies and troops growing every day, all the American Expeditionary Force needed was a powerful leader to command it. They found their man in General John J. Pershing, who at fifty-six was "an imposing figure, tanned, ramrod-straight, and meticulously groomed. This man had presence, and he was all soldier."[4]

Following Pershing to Europe, Patton, 60 officers, and 128 War Department clerks, civilians, and enlisted men left New York City on 28 May 1917 aboard the British steamer HMS *Baltic*.[5] During the voyage, Patton had no specific duties on Pershing's staff and was listed as a line officer. Patton also started his World War I diary on 18 May 1917. While it was not as detailed as his diary in World War II, Patton wrote in it nearly daily. Often it was nothing more than a few lines about what he did that day. Patton had journaled nearly his entire life and would continue to do so up until his death in 1945. When Patton's leading biographer, historian Martin Blumenson, first edited Patton's papers, the two volumes quickly made the best-seller lists. As time wore on, Patton would grow keenly aware he was writing for historians of the future. His World War I diary is much more innocent and offers less insight into his mindset than his diary entries in the 1940s. In World War II, Patton was in the high command, and in a prominent position, and knew he would be studied long after the war ended, but in 1917, Patton was a just a first lieutenant about to be promoted to captain and mainly wrote the diary for himself and his family. To avoid confusion, Patton, once in command of the 1st Tank Brigade, was mandated by the United States Army to keep an official diary of his daily operations. This diary offers very little to historians other than esoteric details of command and offers very few personal observations. In fact, as the war progressed, Patton did not write the official diary. Instead he had a junior officer write it, and Patton would just add his signature and any small edits or additions at the end of the day.

Neither he nor Hugh Drum had specific duties on shipboard, but the two, along with other officers, created the "Baltic Society," which reunited annually to celebrate the crossing of the Atlantic to Liverpool. For most of the voyage Patton kept himself in shape, collected money for war orphans, and worked on his French. In France in 1912—following the Summer Olympics in Stockholm, where Patton represented the United States in the modern pentathlon,[6] finishing a respectable fifth—he had fallen in love with French culture and the language and, while far from fluent, he taught the language on the voyage.

Even General Pershing frequented these lectures. Patton himself wondered how much he helped: "I have worked over five hours a day on French ever since we started and am one of the best on the boat which does not speak well for the others."[7] While the sinking of ships by German U-boats was common during this time, Patton seemed carefree during the uneventful voyage if perhaps relieved when on 6 June 1917 he awoke to find two British destroyers (the *Tucker* and the *Rowan*) on either side of the ship. The next day the passengers spotted land, and finally on 8 June HMS *Baltic* docked at Liverpool to wide celebration, including the playing of "The Star-Spangled Banner" by the Royal Welsh Fusiliers.[8] The first contingent of the American Expeditionary Force had arrived, but before they could fight, much had to be done. The next morning, Patton met with General Pershing and officially began readying the United States Army for entry into World War I.[9] While this preparation ultimately led to Allied victory, Patton, being so close to combat but not actually in the war, was already growing frustrated with his role as a staff officer.

Following the landing in Liverpool, Patton's first assignment was to lead sixty-seven troops to their quarters in the Tower of London. While not particularly thrilled with his assignment and duties, Patton knew that almost every officer back home would trade jobs with him in an instant. (His future friend Dwight D. Eisenhower would never fight overseas in World War I.) Though still far from the front, Patton was closer in London than in Washington, DC, and that whetted his appetite for war somewhat. For the few days spent in London, Patton was kept busy socializing, drinking, and fruitlessly ordering his troops around. After a week of celebrating their arrival, Pershing and his staff left for France. Arriving in Paris around 6 p.m. on 13 June, Patton noted that he had finally gotten his first glimpse of the war as he saw "several train loads of British wounded; they did not look very happy."[10] As he wrote in his diary, since he was promoted to captain he now had the responsibility of managing "38 orderlies. 10 Engineers. 10 Chauffers. 7 Signal Corps. Total 65 enlisted plus 2 Med Crops [sic]."[11] Otherwise, Patton spent a great deal of time perfecting his French language skills. Beatrice Ayer Patton had spent many years in France and was fluent in the language. Patton, a lifelong Francophile, prided himself on his French and continued speaking the language his entire life. It would serve him well once he joined the Tank Corps and had to rely on the French for tanks.

Once again without specific duties, Patton functioned basically as the commander of the headquarters troops. This job entailed commanding guards on duty, making sure there were enough chauffeurs for the automobiles, and making sure the cars were running normally. At this point in his life, and helped by the wealth of the Ayer family, Patton was very familiar with automobiles and motors. Prior to World War I, he had already tinkered with engines and generally loved working on and driving automobiles. His hobby would eventually help his military career, but by the summer of 1917, Patton had yet to even hear about tanks. Continuing the theme of what he thought of his duties, Patton wrote in a letter to his wife Beatrice five days after arriving in France, "Personally I have not got a great deal to do."[12] While his duties did not change, his workload increased, and Patton aptly described his job as "just like commanding a troop, being Adjutant and Q.M. [quartermaster] and Ordinance [sic] officer all at the same time. . . . I would trade jobs with almost any one for any thing."[13] While he hated his job, Patton did the best he could and served well under Pershing, who was often very hard to work for. In a rare criticism of Pershing, Patton wrote to his father about how life was like working for the general:[14] "J. might let me go over but I doubt even that as he is against leaves. In fact I think he works the staff too hard[.] Sunday is just like any other day and if this war is to last three years more as we think that will be more than men can stand. It is true the British staff works all day and every day but a Britisher never works very hard he is less intense than we are so stands it better."[15]

While busy with work, Patton still had time to write almost daily to his wife, and to experience some of the thrills of modern machinery. On 14 June 1917, Patton flew in a plane for the first time. Prior to leaving Pershing's staff, Patton often flew on planes when he could. He wrote to his wife of the first experience that before "see[ing] the flying machines I have never before known what flying was. It is impossible to imagine the perfection which these people have attained."[16] Often the pilot was none other than Colonel Billy Mitchell, who would become one of the great air power theorists (and later court-martialed, partially for his views on air power). While flying in combat and in peacetime were two different things, Patton was open to new ideas and weapons. It was a mentality that would serve him well with tanks in both world wars. And later in World War II Patton was one of the first American generals to understand the significance of combined and coordinated attacks with ground troops and close air support.

He wrote in his diary of that first flight, "I always thought it would frighten me but it did not. One feels perfectly safe and the machine seems as steady as a church."[17] While Patton felt safe in the plane and in Paris, Beatrice Patton often worried about his well-being, and he reassured her rather humorously, unintentionally or not, that he was "a lot safer here than I usually am at home because I don't play polo or race or jump or do any other interesting thing."[18] It is interesting to note that his wife's fear of Patton injuring himself was well placed. Patton was prone to catastrophic and near fatal automobile accidents, falling off horses, and numerous head injuries. During his life, it is likely he had a minimum of ten severe concussions due to falls and accidents. In 1917 there was no concept of concussions or the effect of countless impacts on the brain and head. Patton nearly died a few months after the letter reassuring his wife, when he got into yet another car wreck:

> On the way back between Amiens and Paris I had my usual yearly accident the machine (not mine) in which I was riding ran into a closed R.R. gate and I carelessly put my head through the front window and cut an artery on my left temple and cut a hole at the point of the jaw on the right side about an inch long and deep it missed the carroted artery and jugular and facial nerve about an 1/8 of an inch if it had gotten them I would probably have cashed in but it did not bleed much.[19]

Aside from crashing automobiles, Patton, making use of his experience with them, was constantly busy fixing their engines and belts and such, and telling people how to fix them, and making sure there were enough to go around. Drawing on his wife's wealth, Patton while in Paris purchased a twelve-cylinder, five-passenger Packard worth $4,386, which today would be equivalent to around $90,000.[20] In typical Patton fashion, this enabled him to be seemingly everywhere. It also was a car that turned the heads of many of his superiors and important officers. While this often helped Patton in his career, it sometimes brought him harmful attention from jealous older officers wondering how a young captain could afford such a vehicle. Patton, conscious that he was able to afford the automobile only because of his wife and her family, wrote her the following day, almost asking for forgiveness for such an extravagant purchase.

> I expect you will think me quite crazy but I am not really what I have done is very sane for with out an auto here one is lost and I have a stunt where by I can buy enough gas.
> I had to pay $4200 for the car on account of the high freight rates but after thinking it over I thought it was the best thing to

do. I hope you approve. I will cable you to day to deposit that much money to my credit in some bank then I will draw a check on it. In that way I will save the exchange.[21]

With his fancy new car secured, Patton turned his attention toward getting his wife overseas in some capacity, official or not. Prior to leaving for Europe, Pershing ordered that wives would not be able to accompany their husbands. This was upsetting to the Pattons, mainly because they had been separated for almost a year while Patton was deployed in Mexico. Both Patton and his wife believed this entitled them to special treatment, as most American officers did not participate in the Mexican Punitive Expedition, nor did they arrive with the lead element of the American Expeditionary Force in France. On 19 June 1917, Patton and his wife for the first time began planning to get Beatrice over to France. For the next few months Patton was overly preoccupied with the project, but not wanting to make waves or use Pershing directly, he wrote to his wife, "For very *important reasons* do not think of starting on your trip before the first of August unless you hear from me to the contrary."[22] The couple devised a number of plans to get her overseas. However, the fear of U-boats made Patton hesitant to have her sail directly to France on the more northern route. Toward the end of June he recommended his wife take the southern route from Cuba. He even talked with Pershing directly about Beatrice and Nita Patton, writing, "I had a talk with J. to day about Nita he does not think she should come over and I am inclined to agree with him he has too much on his hands and it would make a bad impression just at present."[23]

It was clear from his diary entries and letters to his wife and other family members that he was talking nearly every day with Pershing about private and family matters. To slip Pershing's name past the censors, the Pattons often would refer to him as "J." or "Nita's suitor." Patton opined in one letter to his wife, "I had a talk for several hours with Nita's suitor we mulled over the past and talked of the future. . . . It will be absolutely wrong for them to get married now or for her to make her proposed trip. Be sure not to encourage her in any way."[24] Patton remarked later in the same letter that Pershing's love for Nita was still strong: "It certainly is the most intense case I have ever seen."[25] It seems that in the summer of 1917, Patton was not especially busy with military duties and filled the time trying to get his wife overseas and making sure Pershing was still planning on marrying his sister.

By July 1917, Patton and Beatrice had another idea: to bring their elder daughter, Beatrice, overseas with her mother. Their younger child, Ruth Ellen, was just a toddler and would stay stateside, but Patton thought "Little B" could travel with her mother.[26] He did press his wife to buy a rubber "safe suit" just in case their ship was attacked by a German U-boat. "They have some sort of rubber garment which is a life preserver and also keeps you dry and hence warm they cost quite a lot but are worth it."[27] The rubber suit supposedly kept its wearer dry and warm in the frigid North Atlantic. It is not clear, but highly unlikely, that Beatrice Patton ever purchased the suit.

Toward the end of July, Patton exhorted his wife numerous times to leave for France. He even went so far as to ask Pershing for permission for Beatrice to head overseas. Pershing declined, and blamed the decision on the Canadians, as Patton related:

> I got your wire asking me to get Gen. P. to give his consent. He can't do it because it was on his advice that the order was issued. You see the British had to send back 60,000 women who came over with the Canadians. . . . Now the only thing to do is put pressure to work on the secretary of state so you can come. Not as a nurse but straight out. . . . I disapprove your coming as a red cross nurse for there is no telling but we would be so far apart we could never meet. Besides you ought to bring little B to keep you company.[28]

It is interesting that Patton, while he desperately wanted his wife to come to France, would not allow her to travel overseas if she was to work for the Red Cross as a nurse. Throughout his time in France, Patton wrote negatively of the Red Cross, repeating to numerous family members that the Red Cross had enough money and did not need more financial donations. Writing to Beatrice in July, Patton warned her: "I think that this Red Cross stuff is largely hysteria and if I were you I would not donate they have a lot more money than they can spend now."[29]

While Patton did not hold the Red Cross or nursing in high esteem, he was not above using the Ayer wealth and donations to get his wife overseas. In an undated letter, likely written at the end of 1917, Patton penned a memo to himself titled "Method of Getting Beatrice to France." In this short letter he laid out a few main points that he thought could help her get approved:

> It seems to me that Mr. Wilson is indepted to Papa more than

he is to the secretary of Treasure Mr. Macadoo [William Gibbs McAdoo]. I feel sure that Col. House would but [put] the matter before the President there are the following excellent reasons B. should be allowed to come.

1. We were separated for eleven months while I was in Mexico.
2. She speaks and writes French like a native having been educated in France.
3. Beatrice and her family have given over $40000.00 to the red cross hence should be entitled to some consideration.

Another point worth considering is the fact that B. unlike most Army women is very rich so there is no possibility of her ever being a tax on the government here.[30]

While Patton had no love for the Red Cross, it was clear he intended to use the massive amounts of money Beatrice's family had donated as a way to get her across the Atlantic.

As the summer of 1917 stretched into August, Patton appeared to fall into a bout of melancholy or depression, having lost hope that Beatrice would be able to travel overseas: "Beatrice you don't know how terribly I feel at not having told you to come right after I did but at the time no one could have forseen the present situation and it seemed better to be sure of conditions here before telling you to come. Then when we first got here it seemed likely that things would be too hot for us and that you had better not come. Now every thing is safe enough so far as our friends the enemy is concerned but the W[ar] D[epartment] is obdurate."[31]

Patton even began to believe many of the rules issued by the United States government and the army had to do with Pershing's relationship with his sister, as he wrote to his wife: "I certainly have the blues over it and don't see just at this moment any help for the trouble either. The absurd part is that we will not be in any real war for a year and would have a chance to see something of our wives. I have a sneaking suspicion that it is for Nita would come that all these laws were made. Though that is hardly just either as there is nothing against the sisters of officers."[32]

By the end of August, Patton still hoped to get his wife to France but was beginning to realize it might have to wait. "I love you and the more I think about your not getting here the worse I feel about it but I keep hoping that things will change for the better and that you will be able to come. I *am sure* you will and I hope and pray it will be soon."[33]

In a sweet and loving letter, which Patton was capable of writing, he added up all the time he had been married but separated and came to the conclusion that between travel, training, the expedition to Mexico, and now World War I, they had been apart for "27.5 months or 2 y[ea]rs 3.5 months."[34]

While some higher-ranking officers managed to get their wives over, either in inventive roles such as Red Cross nurses or State Department employees or in various illegal ways, many men found themselves in trouble with Pershing and with national governments. Although Patton was extremely close with Pershing and attempted mightily to get Beatrice over, both partners were coming to see that it was best for his career if she stayed stateside. Heartbroken, Patton continued to write his beloved wife and wrote some very romantic and sweet letters. "I have been leaving the kissing marks off for fear that they might be misinterpreted [by the censors] as a cipher but you know I mean them anyway."[35] While Martin Blumenson believed he was a womanizer and unfaithful husband during the Second World War, Patton still loved his wife and was attentive throughout their marriage. It is unclear if Patton had a girlfriend or mistress in World War I as many officers did, but if so, he was wise enough never to write about it! Regardless, without Beatrice Patton's guidance, passion, and wealth, Patton would never have achieved the success he did.

The Pattons discussed more plans to get her to France, but by the end of the summer it appeared the two realized there was little they could do without harming his career. They did not drop the subject entirely, it did resurface from time to time, but by the fall of 1917 both accepted that they were likely going to have to wait until the war ended to reunite. While Patton wrote daily to his wife, his personality and attitude, depending on how he felt that morning, could verge on the mean and petty. As numerous wartime letters attested, Patton was terrified not just of himself growing old and gray but of his wife doing so. In October 1917 Patton told his wife, "If you don't get over here try not to worry too much and get gray hair. I don't like them. I put tonic on my head every day and take exercises so as to keep my youthful appearance. You ought to take exercises too a little."[36] Throughout the war, Patton would drop rather obvious hints that he wanted his wife to look no different than before he left. He could be charming at times, and always appeared to realize he had been too mean in certain letters and in following letters would be much kinder, for instance telling her she looked "very pluckie."[37]

Patton was prone on a nearly daily basis to dabble in poetry. His biographer Martin Blumenson, a poet in his own right, did not think highly of Patton's poetry, but Patton wrote often about those around him, including a poem he wrote for his wife while in Mexico titled "To Beatrice":

> Oh! The lovliest of women,
> Whatever I gain or do
> Is naught, if in achieving
> I bring not joy to you
>
> I know I often grieve you
> All earthly folk are frail
> But if this grief I knowing wrought
> My life's desire would fail
>
> The mandates of stern duty
> Oft take us far apart
> But space is impotent to check
> The heart which calls to heart
>
> Perhaps by future hidden
> Some greatness waits in store
> If so, the hope your praise to gain,
> Shall make my efforts more
>
> For victory, apart from you
> Would be an empty gain
> A laurel crown you could not share,
> Would be reward in vain.
>
> You are my inspiration
> Light of my brain and soul
> Your guiding love by night and day
> Will keep my valor whole.[38]

Although he longed for his wife, the tempo of Patton's job increased as American soldiers arrived in larger numbers and the American Expeditionary Force began to grow into a more complex organization. During the summer of 1917, while busy with staff work, Patton's spirit was warmed by his promotion to captain. He was officially promoted in May 1917 but did not receive official notice until later in August.[39] This was a permanent promotion, not a temporary promotion because of the war, but Patton was promoted earlier in recognition of his position on the American Expeditionary Force. While satisfied with the promotion, he was not content. He angrily wrote to his wife and family about reserve officers and their rate of promotion: "The reserve officers we have so far are a mess and as there are a lot of them in the Q.M. it is a great nuisance. They ought never make them higher than lieutenants the majors are insufferable."[40] A few weeks later Patton was upset about his possibility of making major, as he was 113th on the list of captains of cavalry, and wrote: "so the next 500000 ought to make me a major. It is certainly an outrage the way they are making majors and even Colonels out of the 3 months training men and leaving men with 9 years training captains. I don't see what they think they are doing."[41] However, he did allow himself some time to brag to his wife about his new rank, and how "we are getting up in the world of course I save a lot."[42] In reality it was irrelevant how much of his salary he saved, as his family did not rely on Patton's pay but instead on the vast Ayer fortune.

Though he had just been promoted to captain, Patton wrote to his wife that he felt optimistic about his chances of being promoted to major. "All sorts of people are being promoted. . . . I don't think they will get down to making me a major but they will before the end of the war so that will be fine you had better send me some gold leaves."[43] The promotion to major, now as in 1917, is an important elevation in rank and responsibility. As majors, officers for the first time are no longer company grade or strictly tactical-level leaders. Instead they are now field-grade officers and take on a larger responsibility in operational and higher levels of war. They also assume key positions in battalions and brigades as executive officers, and many careers are made or ended at the rank of major. Patton, unfortunately, would have to wait a few more months to make major; however, just as in World War II, that did not prevent him from wearing the rank earlier than he was legally allowed.

Seemingly busy with little to show for it, Patton would often travel with Pershing as his aide-de-camp. On 20 July the two traveled to a meeting with the British commander in chief, Field Marshal Sir Douglas Haig. Prior to their departure, Patton had installed a license plate on the front of their automobile that read "U.S. No 1."[44] As with the Packard that he purchased, Patton made sure that Pershing, and by extension the whole United States Expeditionary Army, was taken seriously and respected as such. During the meeting, Pershing impressed Haig, but overall Haig felt Pershing's staff was rather unspectacular. Yet Haig wrote in his diary after the meeting that "the A.D.C. [aide-de-camp] is a fire-eater and longs for the fray."[45] For Patton, there could have been no greater praise.

While earning praise from Field Marshal Haig and experiencing the thrill of flying in a plane, Patton grew more disgusted with his job. As more of his West Point classmates were promoted to major and lieutenant colonel he began to look for other jobs in other branches. In late July for the first time Patton had a serious conversation about tanks and their role in the war. Although trained as a cavalryman and therefore appreciative of mobile warfare and aggressive tactics, he was less than enthusiastic; "the Tank [is] not worth a damn," he originally thought.[46] Instead Patton stuck with his staff job, but following Pershing's move to Chaumont on 1 September, he grew more frustrated and believed himself to be "nothing but [a] hired flunky. I shall be glad to go back to the line again and will try to do so in the spring. . . . These damn French are bothering us with a lot of details which have nothing to do with any thing. I have a hard time keeping my patience."[47] By late September, Patton began to discuss with his wife the possibility of joining up with tanks.

> There is a lot of talk about "Tanks" here now and I am interested as I can see no future to my present job. The casualties in the Tanks is high that is lots of them get smashed but the people in them are pretty safe as we can be in this war. It will be a long long time yet before we have any [tanks] so don't get worried. We will see each other and talk it over before I will even have a chance to apply. I love you too much to try to get killed but also too much to be willing to sit on my tail and do nothing.[48]

Also in September, Patton, along with Fox Conner, who would become one of Pershing's most trusted and accomplished subordinates, and other American Expeditionary Force staff officers, moved to Fontainebleau, in a forest south of Paris. Patton enjoyed the new living conditions and remarked to his wife about the house, "We have a very nice house with two floors as I am the lowest ranking I live on the third and my room is quite small with a lot of bras and gilt affairs in it."[49] While this meant Patton was one step closer to the war, he was very much reminded of how safe he was in his staff position. His relative safety began to eat at Patton. He wanted to break away from Pershing and get into the fight. Before that could happen, though, the United States Army had to grow, and Patton was still a small part of the machine.

This is not to say he was not busy. When Patton wrote out his daily schedule, it showed he was generally up and riding from 8 to 9 a.m. Then he inspected barracks and kitchens from 9 to 10, and then a "thousand and one things from 1:30 to seven drill the clearks."[50] After his duties were done, he ate dinner at 7 p.m. and read until bed at about 10:30. It was around this time that Patton became increasingly disenchanted with his role and position on Pershing's staff. His letters home to Beatrice changed during the fall. No longer trying to get her overseas, Patton became depressed about what the next step in his career should be. He wanted to get into combat and wanted to get a position that would enable him to gain rank and notoriety. But still, by the fall of 1917 the United States Army was just not ready for independent combat, and Patton complained to his wife, "This war would be a lot more interesting if we could have some fighting but as it is this everlasting getting ready gets tiresome and I fear we will be at it a long time yet before we do any killing."[51]

Seemingly aware that he was prone to depression, Patton followed up with a letter explaining why he was so melancholy:

I was very low in my mind yesterday there seemed no future to my job and I was disgusted with the daily grind. Last night we had a promotion party for the Gen. and all the officers were there after the show the Gen called me and said he was about to recommend some promotions in the national army and I would like to be a major of cavalry or any other branch or staff department. . . . As I have said the only chance for a man of my age is to command troops. . . . The Tanks are yet in an unsettled state but they may have a great future. I have consulted Col Malone and am waiting for Col Eltinge to get home to talk to him. I will write you what I decide.[52]

Though at first he was skeptical of tanks, it seems that the boredom and safety of staff duty was too much for him to deal with, and his lust for glory drove Patton to join the tanks. By early October, Patton met and talked with Colonel LeRoy Eltinge, one of the leading officers on Pershing's staff, about the role of tanks and whether Patton should join them. "Col. Eltinge asked me if I wanted be a Tank officer. I said yes and also talked the matter over with Col. McCoy who advised me to write a letter asking that in the event of Tanks being organized that my name be considered."[53] On 3 October 1917, Patton submitted to the Tank Service (later called Tank Corps) a letter outlining his cavalry background, his mechanical ability, and his fluency in French that made him the right man for the job. Perhaps, Patton wrote, the most important reason was, "I believe that I am the only American who has ever made an attack in a motor vehicle."[54] Writing about his experience during the Mexican Punitive Expedition, Patton was showing his usual flair for self-promotion.

While waiting for an answer about tanks, Patton was sent to the hospital with a case of jaundice. To his concerned wife he wrote: "I am loosing [sic] a little of my fine yellow coller but still look very funny and yellow."[55] During his hospital stay, which reached into November, Patton debated his decision internally. Should he go with tanks? Infantry? Or should he stay in his role as a staff officer? The decision was really between going to the infantry and going with the untested tanks. For Patton, there was really no debate about staying a staff officer. He wanted to command men in combat, and he realized he had a better shot at higher rank through field command. Patton was skeptical of joining a new branch of service and was unsure if American tanks would ever make it into the fight. The benefit of joining the United States Tank Service was he would be among the first officers in the new branch and could potentially benefit from being one of the select few. On the other hand, joining the infantry would assure Patton of command and combat. As an infantry officer, however, he would be one of thousands and would have a harder time distinguishing himself in combat. On 18 October, when Patton wrote in his diary about his decision, it is clear he was still very unsure about what to do, but he had discussed the decision with Colonel Eltinge. "I talked Tank with him and decided to try to become a Maj of Inft. Next night Oct 18 Col Elitnge came and said Gen McAndrew wanted to start a Tank school at Langres on Nov 15 and would I take it. Inspite of my resolution to the contrary I said yes. But I kept discussing it pro and con with Col F. Conner and again decided on Inft."[56]

Patton admitted later in his diary entry that he "did not sleep a bit that night and decided to try the Tanks as it aperes the way to high command if I make a go of it."[57]

It is not clear precisely when Patton made up his mind to join the Tank Service, but by the end of October he was committed to the new-fangled service. Finally on 10 November 1917 Patton was officially chosen for the Tank Service and was ordered to prepare a School for Light Tanks. With Colonel (later General) Eltinge selected to head all tanks, heavy and light, Patton wrote to his father of his "golden dream":

Here is the golden dream. 1st. I will run the school 2 then they will organise a battalion I will command it 3. Then if I make

good and the T. do and the war lasts I will get the first regiment.
4. With the same "IF" as before they will make a brigade and I
will get the star. . . . Also the T. will be a great drawing card in
the papers and illustrated magazines. The casualties in the tanks
is about 25% but in the crews only about 7½% which is much
lower than the Dough boys also in the tanks you are not apt to
be wounded you either get blown to bitts by a direct hit or you
are not touched.[58]

Remarkably, Patton had laid out basically what would happen to him
the following year. He would run the first United States Tank School, he
would eventually command the first United States Tank Brigade in United
States history, and he would play an important role in the reduction of
the St. Mihiel salient and the Meuse-Argonne campaign. Patton got only
one prediction wrong: he would not wear the star of a brigadier general;
instead he would fall just short, reaching the rank of colonel.

With orders in hand, Patton wrote his last diary entry as a staff officer: "This is [my] last day as staff officer. Now I rise or fall on my own.
'God judge the right.'"[59] Patton would rise, and his duty with the tanks
would bring him fame, honor, and glory in battle.

2

Land Crabs, Land Ironclads, Landships

The Tank

The tanks are yet in an unsettled state but they may have a great future.
— Patton to Beatrice Patton, 9 October 1917

Throughout the history of warfare, weapons have been envisioned to defeat the enemy without endangering the lives of those using them. An early example is the wooden Trojan Horse, which could be seen as the first armored weapon. In 1838 an English commoner by the name of John George wrote a petition to the House of Commons announcing himself as the sole inventor of a "modern steam war chariot" that would prove "very destructive in case of war."[1] The machine would be operated by three men, would be safe behind armor, and would cut through the deepest of military lines. Like most governments, which are skeptical of everything from common citizens, the House of Commons rejected the plan. Even in 1838 men were beginning to design and build what Brevet Colonel J. F. C. Fuller would call the "trinity of trench, machine gun and wire."[2]

In 1914 a British officer, Colonel Ernest D. Swinton, on hearing of an American Holt caterpillar tractor "which could climb like the devil,"[3] began to think of a weapon for use in the war, and that idea was a "self-propelled vehicle, capable of crossing trenches and so armored as to be impervious to machine-gun bullets."[4] Luckily for the British government, this idea was first brought to Winston Churchill, then First Lord of the Admiralty, who unlike most British government officials believed in original ideas and fresh thinking. To steal a modern term used by American army officers, Churchill was prone to "good idea fairies," meaning he would have great ideas pop up in his head, and he was in a position to execute them and see them through, often unchecked by superiors or other officials. These good ideas could lead to disastrous results, as Gallipoli would show in World War I, and later the amphibious landing of Anzio in Italy during World War II. However, the tank was one of his better ideas! By 1915, under Churchill's urging, the British navy formed the Admiralty Landships Committee.[5] To hide the development of the "landcruisers," the new weapon was code-named "tank."[6]

After a year of hard work in design and production, a prototype was ready, and on 29 January 1916 the machine, dubbed HMS *Centipede* or "Mother," gave its first demonstration to men such as Prime Minister David Lloyd George and Arthur Balfour, who had replaced Churchill as First Lord of the Admiralty.[7] Initial thoughts on the tank varied from person to person. Balfour was said to have "demonstrated a childlike pleasure" in the new weapon, while Secretary of State for War Lord Kitchener believed the tank to be nothing more than a "pretty mechanical toy."[8] This would be a remarkably common reaction among senior officials during World War I. More traditional leaders tended to shy away from tanks and had good reason to disregard them. They were prone to mechanical failure, were generally unproven in the field, and were extremely expensive. Other leaders, often younger or more willing to try anything to end the ghastly carnage, saw the tanks, while technically and mechanically troublesome, as a way to change the war and enable infantry to get closer to the enemy and make it through no-man's-land. For those leaders, who would include George S. Patton, the tank still needed to be developed, but it was something that could change the entire character of war. Whatever the reactions, the tank performed well enough that it was rushed into production and made ready for combat.

While the British invented the tank, the French were not too far behind. The French believed that tanks should be more offensive weapons—not the mechanical infantry that some later in the war would argue for, but a weapon that could not only get soldiers across trenches and no-man's-land but could also take out German machine-gun nests. They did not discount the defensive potential of tanks, especially their first two models. But as the French Renault would show the French and American forces in 1918, light tanks were much better suited for offensive operations in certain terrain, while the heavier British tanks were better able to exploit the gains made by infantry and lighter tanks. The British, for their part, wanted tanks to be more armored carriers of infantry troops. This difference in objective led to the creation of different tanks. The British built the thirty-ton Mark I,[9] which was able to deflect German fire but was generally too large for the often wet and muddy fields of Europe. During the war, the British heavies were apt to get stuck in the mud or trenches. The French were more concerned with speed and mobility. They developed three tanks, the Schneider, the St. Chamond, and the Renault.[10] The St. Chamond, with a 75-millimeter gun, needed a nine-person crew to operate it and weighed nearly twenty-three tons.[11] The Schneider needed only six men, and it too had a 75-millimeter gun. The main difference between the two was that the Schneider weighed only fifteen tons, far less than the St. Chamond and the British Mark I.[12] Other tanks such as the Renault Char FT (for *faible tonnage*, or light weight)[13] were two-man carriers with a smaller 37-millimeter gun and weighed just a little over seven tons. The Renault would be the light tank of choice for the American Expeditionary Force, and it served admirably in the war. While the tanks of World War I were primitive and prone to failure, they did have an important effect on the war and ultimately helped the Allies win.

With both light and heavy tanks, the British and French each had their own tactical concepts for tank warfare. The British were correct in believing that tanks should be active fighters, yet the design of the Mark I and its later models prevented them from being used in some operations. While armed with a powerful gun and immense armor, the Mark I was too heavy for its own good and, as mentioned, often got stuck or suffered mechanical failure before it could attack and make a difference in battle. As for the French, they were correct about mobility being important, but they did not give enough offensive power to their tanks. While the Schneider and St. Chamond had 75-millimeter guns, the barrel was often too short to create a powerful blast, and its limited rotation hindered its effectiveness. For all the tanks in World War I, the drivers' sight lines were poor, and this led to more tank officer casualties than anticipated in 1915 and 1916, as officers generally had to lead their tanks on foot, exposed to the gas and machine-gun fire of the Germans. The Renault, while the quickest of the tanks, was not the fastest, and with only a small 37-millimeter gun or an 8-millimeter machine gun, it was mainly ineffective against defensive works heavier than machine-gun nests. However, it was very effective in taking out German machine gunners, and Patton would make this a key task in his brigade and in his training of the United States Tank Corps. It seems both sides had a valid concept, but tactically it often takes years for doctrine and training to adapt to new weapons and weapon systems. The tank, like the machine gun, chemical weapons, and indirect fire of artillery, was what historians and military leaders call a revolution in military affairs, or an RMA. Though not always technologically driven, most focus on new weapons of the day to defeat their current adversaries. The issue with this concept, historically, is that the nation or army with the newest toys does not always win. Often it takes another power to understand the new weapon's inherent strengths and weaknesses and adapt them to a new organization or training model. Instances have been seen throughout the history of war. Maurice of Nassau and the Dutch were not the first to use gunpowder weapons, but Maurice was the first to effectively mass them and incorporate them with his pikeman to great effect. Gustavus Adolphus would follow Nassau's lead in the Thirty Years' War by adding more muskets and making his lines more linear. This tradition persisted in World War I, and as the war continued, both combatants were forced to deal with new RMAs. For the Western Allies, the tank was just an extension of this tradition and another complex problem to solve. Among the major challenges for the first generation of tanks were maintenance issues and gasoline supply. Fortunately for the Allies, they had enough tanks to fill in for those that broke down, and when it mattered most, they could throw a sufficient number at the enemy. As for gas, they would experiment with a variety of ideas, but logistical support for tanks did not fully mature until well into the interwar period and even World War II.

For the brave men who fought in tanks throughout World War I, design flaws proved harder to overcome than the enemy. More often than not, tanks were knocked out of action by poor design or mechanical failure rather than by German attacks. Small-arms fire generally caused little damage to tanks, although by 1918 the Germans had adapted some of their artillery and developed antitank weapons that could completely destroy a tank and its crew.

Historically, the first man to face action in a tank was Basil Henriques. Standing more than six feet three inches, extremely tall for this era, Henriques somehow managed to wedge himself into his small "female" tank,[14] and with two other tanks he set off for the village of Morval. By the time they arrived, the tanks were exhausted and had suffered numerous "wounds." Traveling across rough terrain, Henriques's tank had its periscope shot off, leaving him blind. Worst of all, armor-piercing bullets were breaking through the supposedly impregnable armor, hitting the driver and gunner.[15] Instead of foolishly moving forward, Henriques ordered the tank back to the British line and jumped out with bloody wounds to his legs and face. The first tank "attack" took a massive toll on Henriques and his company. Another officer went mad from the experience and killed himself, and others suffered nervous breakdowns.[16]

If Basil Henriques's adventure was a horrid start for the tank, its first major engagement was just as bad. Not even two years from design to production, the tank was sent into action in serious numbers on 15 September 1916 in the Battle of the Somme. Forty-nine Mark I tanks moved individually to the front during the night, and before even reaching their attack line, seventeen had broken down.[17] For the tanks and their crews, the start was an ominous sign of what to come. When at dawn the tanks finally attacked, many became stuck in the mud, but a few broke through and helped the infantry in their objectives. While the attack was far from an overwhelming success, the tanks did create fear in the German soldiers and High Command. The German soldiers' first impression of the tank was reflected in their cry of "The devil is coming!"[18] More important, the tanks sent a shock wave through the German High Command, which immediately issued a stand-fast order. Regardless of the direct impact of the tank, the Battle of the Somme had ushered in a new era, an era in which armored vehicles would forever change the way war was fought. Just as during its development, senior military leaders and government officials were divided on the future of the tank. However, the necessity of ending the war meant tanks were here for the duration.

While the Battle of the Somme began a new era in warfare, tanks were still seen as novelty toys that had yet to prove their value. This all changed on 20 November 1917 at 6:20 a.m., when 378 tanks surprised German defenses at Cambrai, a small city in northern France.[19] The attack was designed by British officer and foremost tank expert J. F. C. Fuller to be a "raid," which hoped to blow a large hole along the six-mile front.[20] Fuller, one of the first proponents of tank warfare and by far the most revolutionary and radical theorist of tank tactics, believed that for the first time tanks had a chance to succeed. Cambrai was selected as the point of attack for three reasons. First, the terrain was perfect for tanks, which at previous battles had been expected to drudge through miles of mud. Second, Cambrai had been quiet for some time, allowing for a surprise attack. Third and most important, the attack was the first battle in which tanks were used in a mass attack rather than as an adjunct to infantry.[21] In six hours the tanks advanced four miles, which could have cost infantry troops months to do, with hundreds of thousands killed. While 179 tanks were lost, a majority from mechanical failure, the attack was an overwhelming success. Unfortunately, Field Marshal Sir Douglas Haig and the British High Command believed the attack so successful that Haig ordered it to continue. By now the tanks and their crews were hopelessly exhausted, and the Germans eventually pushed the attackers back.

Although the battle is considered a tactical stalemate, the attack proved to many on both sides that if tanks were deployed en masse and on suitable ground, they could change the path of the war, perhaps even ending it. The impact of Cambrai was not immediately felt, but in one day the vaunted Hindenburg Line was broken and more than eight thousand Germans were captured. Perhaps J. F. C. Fuller put it best when after the battle he said that Cambrai "tolled out an old tactics and rang in a new."[22] As Cambrai played out, George S. Patton Jr. was following the battle intently and was overjoyed with the tanks' success.

For Patton, the success at Cambrai not only justified his decision to switch to tanks, it also brought him much publicity as the first tanker in United States Army history. "Since the English success the other day," he wrote to his wife, "lots of people have suddenly discovered that in the tanks they have always had faith and now express a desire to accept the command of them but fortunately I beat them to it by four days."[23] With his career move vindicated, Patton felt relieved but knew that the hard work was yet to come.

Patton still had time to brag about his luck and new position, writing to his wife on 9 November:

What do you think of me I am detailed in charge of the School for Light Tanks. To begin with I will have to go to the French Tank school for two weeks then to the Factory for a week then start the school at a Town about twenty miles from here. . . . I did not mention the tanks much before as I feared it might not come out but if it works I have pulled one of the biggest coups of my life so far. If it don't I will not have lost much for all the schools are at the town I am going to and I will be able to take some courses at the staff college.

He ended the letter by telling Beatrice, "Don't mention what I told you to many people and don't talk of light Tanks they are more or less a secret. Simply say Tanks."[24] Operational security was not a focus for the United States Army and George S. Patton!

Before heading to the Tank Corps, Patton, still a staff officer under Pershing, wrote a memo on 12 November 1917 on appearance and saluting. While much has been written about Patton's attention to cleanliness, neatness, and military appearance in World War II, it is notable that he developed his reputation as a stern disciplinarian in World War I. This focus on detail was not without purpose to Patton. He understood, perhaps better than most officers in the American Expeditionary Force, that they represented the elite and best of not just the United States Army but also the entire nation. He was particularly fearful of American officers and soldiers looking disheveled or unprofessional. He wanted the European allies, who still held the United States Army and its history in low regard, to see how well trained and professional the American officer and soldier was. For Patton, appearance was not everything, but it was a major point of focus and one he did not intend to relax on. This is particularly vital when nations and armies go to war. Often, especially in total wars like both world wars, certain standards that would be enforced in peacetime are no longer deemed important or valuable. Officers no longer worry about uniform infractions, physical training, or the small administrative tasks that lend themselves to healthy organizations as large as army units. When winning the war is key, standards fall by the wayside. For Patton and Pershing, this was unacceptable for the leading contingent of American army officers in France. This issue with standards in wartime is not unique to the Americans or to World War I. The United States Army in the wars in Afghanistan and Iraq has had to deal with it for years. While the major problems often do not appear in wartime but only when the fighting ends and the force returns to garrison duty, they are largely due to a lack of enforcing standards during war. Officers and soldiers develop bad habits, and they are hard to break once the unit's soldiers return home. Patton and Pershing were well aware of lowering standards, especially among the growing numbers of new soldiers and officers. Ever since he arrived in Europe, Patton had been upset with reserve officers and the general appearance of American military officers. Throughout his career Patton had particular contempt for reserve or newly created officers. While some were not good officers, his main issue with the reservists was they were often promoted ahead of him, and for that alone they deserved extra attention!

In the memo he laid out what he had seen and what needed to be corrected:

1. Personal observation leads me to the opinion that some of the officers on duty at these Headquarters do not compare favorably with either the enlisted men or some of the Field Clearks in the matter of saluting and in dress.
2. I have had frequent occasion to correct lieutenants and captains for failing to salute me or for saluting in a slovenly manner using only one or two fingers . . . It is most discouraging to a soldier to

turnout a snappy salute to an officer and have it answered by a casual wave of the hand.
3. Neatness. There is in my opinion a decided lack of neatness on the part of some officers in so far as the condition of their uniform and equipment goes.
4. The preceding remarks apply to new officers of all ranks but there are some regular officers who could be more exact in the same details.[25]

Patton's attention to detail is remarkable to average-to-below-average officers, but Patton understood his boss and understood that Pershing viewed standards and correctness in the same manner. Patton would continue this close attention to detail during the interwar period and in World War II. Cultivating it in World War I would help make Patton a great field commander. When officers focus on the little things, it echoes down the entire unit to the lowest private. This is what made Pershing and Patton such great officers, both in peacetime and in war. Now, did that mean it was always a pleasurable experience to work for Patton? No, but such is life in the United States Army.

On 19 November Patton left Paris to see his first tank factory. The impression it left on him is hard to describe, as he wrote only a short sentence in his diary, saying that the tanks he observed "seem fine."[26] He was much more emphatic about tanks after driving one for the first time and wrote to his wife in glowing terms of their fun and potential:

I drove a Tank to day it is easy to do after an auto and quite comfortable though you can see nothing at all there are three little slits about this size [here a drawing]. The man in the turret can see a little more but not much they go about as fast as one can run and turn like lightning. It is funny to hit small trees and see them go down. They are noisy but easy riding they rear up like a horse or stand on their head with perfect impunity.

I have also fired a gun from the turret both still and while moving I really think they are very useful.[27]

Patton's first assignment in the Tank Corps was to learn as much about the tank as possible, not just how to drive it but how it works and what it can and cannot do. In order to begin the American Expeditionary Force Light Tank School, Patton along with twenty-eight-year-old Lieutenant Elgin Braine was sent to visit the French tank training center at Champlieu in the Forest of Compiègne for two weeks, followed by one week at a tank factory in the Paris suburb of Billancourt. Elgin Braine, a reserve officer originally assigned to the 1st United States Infantry Division, was ordered to serve under Patton because of his mechanical and technical knowledge. Familiarity with machines was a key factor in gaining a position in the newly created United States Tank Corps. It is good to remember that automobiles were still in their infancy and most soldiers in the war had little to no experience with them. While knowing nothing of tanks, Patton had in Braine the immense talent of a mechanical engineer who until the end of the war provided a valuable assist in getting Patton's orders and tank specifications through the bureaucratic mess of the United States military.

During their weeks studying French light tanks, Patton and Braine made four suggestions that were eventually adopted: a self-starter, improvements to the fuel tank to protect against gas leaks, an interchangeable mount that allowed the tank to carry a 37-millimeter cannon or a machine gun, and finally a speaking tube to allow the tankers to talk over the sound of the engine.[28] Also it was while at Champlieu that Patton drove his first tank, a French Renault. His impression that it was easy to control, and that anyone with driving experience could operate the Renault, left Patton extremely happy with the tank and confident he had made the correct decision.

After three weeks of intensive study and breaking tanks apart, Patton and Braine began the process of creating the Light Tank School. Before this could happen, the Tank Corps first had to decide what tanks to use. Following a fact-finding mission, the United States War Department decided on the Mark VII as their heavy tank. The American version, named the Mark VIII, a close model of the British heavy tank, weighed a massive 43.5 tons, had an eleven-man crew, and achieved a dizzying maximum speed of 6.5 miles per hour.[29] For the light tank, the United States chose to copy the French Renault, which tank specialist J. F. C. Fuller correctly wrote was "nothing more than cleverly made mountings for machine guns."[30] The American version of the Renault would weigh only 6.5 tons, with a maximum speed of 5.5 miles per hour, and needed only a two-man crew to operate it.[31] As regards the light tanks, the Americans, much influenced by Patton's ideas on the subject, aligned their tank theory with the French and wanted the tanks to be more than just infantry carriers.

Patton liked the Renault, mainly for its mobility and quickness. Compared to the the British Mark-numbered models, it was also much more reliable. While the tanks of World War I were nothing like the modern tanks that emerged by the 1940s when it came to reliability, for World War I the Renault was as reliable as a tank could be! The two-man crew consisted of a gunner, usually a sergeant, and a driver, usually a corporal. Each tank had either a 37-millimeter cannon or a French Hotchkiss 8-millimeter machine gun.[32]

Communicating inside the tanks proved difficult at best. Completely closed in, with little light seeping through, early tankers devised a way to communicate. Unable to talk because of the noisy engines, the gunner would kick the driver in the back of the head to go forward, a kick on top of his head was the signal to stop, and a kick on either right or left shoulder was to go right or left.[33] Prior to the use of radio communication, this was the best the tankers could do, and amazingly they were able to operate in this fashion.

With a heavy and light tank selected, the United States Tank Corps now had to organize and produce the tanks. General Pershing decided that the United States Tank Corps would consist of five heavy battalions, later doubled to ten heavy battalions, and twenty light tank battalions.[34] Following Colonel Eltinge's suggestion, between 375 and 600 heavy tanks and 1,200 to 1,500 light tanks were required.[35] Unfortunately for the Americans, manufactures at home were ill prepared for the large task ahead, and on Armistice Day there were around 23,000 tanks on order, but only 26 ever arrived in Europe, after the war was over.[36] In order to supply the American Expeditionary Force with tanks, the United States and Pershing reached an agreement with the Supreme War Council and Allied commander in chief Marshal Foch on 17 August 1918 for light and heavy tanks.[37] Though the tanks were on order from the British and French, it would be a few months until Patton's Light Tank School would even see a tank.

With tanks promised to the Americans, the Tank Corps now had to grow from Patton and Elgin Braine to a full operating branch of the AEF. Colonel (later General) Samuel D. Rockenbach was formally appointed chief of the Tank Corps on 22 December 1917. Rockenbach, a graduate of Virginia Military Institute, was twenty-two years older than Patton and his opposite in almost every way. A stoic and even-tempered figure, Rockenbach lacked a sense of humor and was chosen not for his great mind but for his work ethic and fairly successful prewar career. When his wife Emma was asked why she chose to marry such a normal, common army officer, she simply replied, "I married him for his conformation, of course. Did you ever see a finer piece of man-flesh?"[38] Rockenbach's official duties included direct command of heavy tanks and Patton's light tanks.[39] Also, Rockenbach worked as a staff officer on all tank issues on Pershing's staff.[40] Almost immediately Patton and Rockenbach's relationship was a very rocky one, and Patton's first reaction on meeting his new boss was extremely rough on the senior commander. "I hope I can make a success of this business but starting with nothing is hard after we get a little nucleus it will go easier. Now I feel helpless and almost beaten but I will make a go of it or bust Rockenbach or no."[41]

Though the two men never became friends, following their service together they had a healthy mutual respect and even grew to admire one another. Still, their relationship was never very easy. During the war, Patton seldom if ever offered Rockenbach any praise; instead he did his best to ignore his boss and stay out of his way. The more mature and emotionally stable Rockenbach never wrote as much as Patton, but he held Patton in higher regard than Patton held him.

Rockenbach is a fascinating figure and played a key role in the creation of the United States Tank Corps. He has still never received the credit for his role in World War I and the development of the tank. Rockenbach traveled to England with Patton as a member of Pershing's staff and was a member of the Baltic Society. Much older and senior in rank, there is little evidence he talked much at all with Patton during their voyage to Europe. He was originally assigned as a quartermaster officer, and Colonel H. W. Brewster wrote a memo soon after their arrival in July 1917 that praised Rockenbach's handling of the landing party, stating that he "performed the duties of Landing Officer, Railway Transportation Officer, and has besides charge of camp arrangements at the time. His landing work was very well carried out; he impressed me as being very energetic and knew the details of his work."[42]

By the end of 1917, Rockenbach was in the running to lead the newly created United States Tank Corps, and he took over the position on 18 January 1918. His first order of business was to proceed to England "for the purpose of getting in touch with the British officials in charge of the Tank Service and to inspect the shops and schools pertaining to that service."[43] Rockenbach and Patton worked closely together in the creation of the corps. As in World War II, where he would clash with his superiors, Patton was in the ideal position for his skills and personality. While Patton had little care or inclination for diplomacy and politics, Rockenbach's cool demeanor helped not only the United States Army but also Patton. It is not clear if Patton ever understood how successful Rockenbach was at his job, especially at keeping bureaucratic wrangling out of

Patton's command. Nowhere is this seen better than in the pivotal and delicate role Rockenbach played in not only the Inter-Allied Tank Committee but the Western alliance.

The Inter-Allied Tank Committee was a small body of officers from Great Britain, France, Italy, and the United States. The chair was Major General Jean Baptiste Estienne, the father of the tank corps in the French army. Major General Sir John Edward Capper represented the British, and the Italians, by far the weakest member of the committee, were led by a Lieutenant Colonel Gorgiulo. As the minutes of the meetings show, Gorgiulo rarely spoke up and played no major role. It appeared he was there more for political reasons and for show than actually planning and winning the war. Rockenbach, who joined the committee in May 1918 as a Colonel, proved to be a skilled hand at diplomacy and negotiating. Junior to Estienne and Capper, he was very vocal in the meetings and spoke always in a professional tone. While Estienne and Capper talked the most, Rockenbach was very efficient when he spoke up.

The committee was important for several reasons. It was designed not just to discuss tank tactics and tank theory but to provide the United States Army with tanks in which to train and ultimately fight. The group also attempted to standardize tanks and tank organizations. In May 1918, following the British success at Cambrai, the committee agreed tanks were going to have a pivotal role in the Great War, but also in future conflicts. While Estienne and Capper often argued over theory, Rockenbach was much more realistic and more focused on the current fight, concerned with getting tanks so his force could eventually join the fray.

The minutes and details of the meetings often focus on theory, but key decisions were made there. While all members of the committee were bullish on tanks, for the Battle of Cambrai had shown, according to Capper, "that by the use of tanks it was possible to break through the enemy lines with a great saving of infantry,"[44] they did not believe tanks were quite ready to replace the artillery and infantry branches of their militaries. The tank committee mainly focused on three tasks: tank organization, tank tactics, and tank manufacturing. The biggest disagreement within the committee was generally over the use of heavy tanks. This argument, in many ways, goes back to the beginning of tank development. The British were always proponents of heavy tanks, again viewing them as infantry carriers, while the French focused on light tanks and viewed tanks as mobile infantry. During World War I, tanks were organized into three groups, heavy, medium, and light. The British focused mainly on heavy tanks of the Mark series, while the French built light tanks such as the Renault tank. The French St. Chamond and Schneider were considered medium tanks, but they were more motorized infantry carriers than tanks. When Patton commanded them later in the war, he regarded them as the weakest unit of his brigade and generally ignored them. The committee believed that light tanks should be allotted to all divisions, but heavy tanks should be used sparingly and only for break-thoughs.[45] As always, many of the military decisions made by the committee were based on their superiors' views and orders, financial cost, and political pressures.

The committee also argued over the relationship of tanks and infantry. This debate would continue during the interwar period, but during World War I nearly all tank officers in the Allied powers believed that the tank had to be supported by the infantry. Patton was no different in this. Part of the Tank Corps's "inferiority complex" was they did not want to alienate the long-established and powerful infantry and cavalry branches. Politically, Patton was no Billy Mitchell. He would never publicly advocate for a separate and independent tank corps as Mitchell would for air power. Privately, by the end of World War I, Patton believed the future of tanks was a separate and distinct branch, just like artillery and infantry, but he was too concerned with his promotion opportunities to state his beliefs openly. The second reason tankers tended to side with the infantry was, tanks were not quite reliable or sturdy enough vehicles to operate independently. They were slow, lumbering, prone to breaking down, and needed the infantry for support. Patton wrote to Rockenbach in May 1918 following the first Inter-Allied Tank Committee meeting:

In considering an operation of tanks and infantry, it is necessary to always bear in mind two very patent but not the less frequently neglected truths. Namely: The advance of Infantry is limited in the last analysis by the physical endurance of the men. The advance of tanks by obstacles incident to the terrain, hence it will be futile to try an attack with infantry and tanks where the ground renders the tanks impotent. From the above statement it is evident that the liaison between the tanks and infantry must be of the closest. It must be worked out in the most minute detail for so complex is its nature that hazy ideas or ill digested plans will become abortive or ruinous in the excitement of the close fighting where the cooperation must be put into practice.[46]

After their first meetings in May 1918, the committee recommended the following organization and dispersement of tanks. The French would be equipped with 800 heavy tanks and 3,000 light tanks.[47] Estienne decided against the French having any medium tanks. The British would get 1,000 heavy tanks, 820 medium tanks, and 1,500 light tanks. The United States, which had no tanks whatsoever in May 1918, was to receive 2,000 heavy tanks and 4,000 light tanks.[48] Like the French, Rockenbach did not view medium tanks favorably. The British agreed to furnish their Allied partners with both heavy and medium tanks, while the French and Americans would build and sell light tanks.

Rockenbach, as chief of the United States Tank Corps, had two main missions as a member of the tank committee: first, to get the United States tanks from their allies, and second, to assure the British and French that the United States would manufacture tanks and support the growing Allied corps. Rockenbach assured his partners that American manufactures would have 6,000 Franco-American Renault light tanks and 1,500 Mark VIII Heavy or so-called Liberty tanks in production by the end of 1918.[49] While this reassured his colleagues in May 1918, the United States would greatly miss the production goals set by Rockenbach. This is not a criticism of Rockenbach, who was in France during the war; the fault lay mainly with United States Army bureaucracy and manufacture mismanagement.

A second issue that plagued the Americans was the United States Army Air Service. Rockenbach and the United States had agreed to build 50 percent of the tanks, mainly the engine, chassis, and transmission, while the rest of the tank would be built and pieced together by the British at their factory in central France at Châteauroux.[50] However, with the rapid expansion of air power, the United States unilaterally made the decision later in 1918 to cancel the Liberty motor and gave many of the engines originally destined for tanks to the air corps.[51] This greatly upset the British and French, but there was little they could do to change the minds of the United States government this late in the war. Additionally, while the Americans had yet to enter the fight, it was clear they were becoming the senior partner in the alliance, especially since the British and French owed billions to the Americans. However, much of this was a moot point as, even with British and French tank designs, the first American-built tanks would not arrive until the war was over.

Rockenbach was more successful acquiring tanks than getting the American government and American companies to manufacture them.

During their first meeting on 6 May 1918, Rockenbach requested that the French provide his infant tank corps with 100 Renault tanks. Estienne rejected the request without hesitation.[52] However, the next day the committee agreed to provide the Americans and Italians with a handful of tanks: "France undertakes to supply in about 10 days 15 Renault tanks to America: in 1 month, 10 Renault tanks to Great Britain. The delivery of the additional 75 Renault tanks promised to American will be considered as soon as the present battle situation allows. The Italian Government will be allotted 5 light tanks for experimental purposes within a month: the balance of 45 will be supplied when conditions allow."[53] This was a major victory for Rockenbach, the Tank Corps, and George S. Patton. The United States was finally going to get tanks!

The Inter-Allied Tank Committee met again in June and again in July 1918. In July, Rockenbach confirmed that the United States Tank Corps would comprise five heavy tank battalions with 340 officers and 3,890 men, and there would be twenty light tank battalions with 400 officers and 7,500 soldiers. With support units attached, the United States Tank Corps would consist of some twenty-five battalions and roughly 750 officers and 15,583 enlisted personnel.[54] Rockenbach hoped that by 1919 the Tank Corps would have five more heavy tank battalions and more than 20,000 soldiers.[55]

Patton had little use for the Inter-Allied Tank Committee, writing in May 1918 that "the Inter-Allied Tank Committee is a nuisance and if it must be used, should only be used as a supply depot. All other questions should be handled in the office, of the Chief of Tank Corps."[56] However, the committee played a pivotal role in the growth of armored warfare, and it was the committee that provided the United States with its first tanks to train on. Patton, as he would show in World War II, had little patience with negotiations with the British and French and viewed the war through the eyes of American policies and positions only. Right or wrong, Patton was not by intellect or personality suited for Rockenbach's position as chief of the Tank Corps. He was, however, much more forward thinking and visionary in regard to the future of tanks, while Rockenbach was better equipped for his administrative and organizational leadership position in the American Expeditionary Force. The two worked well together in their positions, but despite his lust for rank, Patton was in the best position for his talents. He was an excellent trainer and thinker when it came to tanks. Nowhere is this better seen than in his initial tank report.

With the United States Tank Corps now organized and ready to begin training, Patton wrote a paper on light tanks, light tank warfare, history, and theory. Submitted in December 1917, the fifty-eight-page report includes a handwritten message from Patton, likely added after the war had ended, that read: "Note—In my opinion this is the basic tank concepts of the US Army. *Very important.*"[57] Patton's tank report is a remarkable achievement in its clarity, vision, and understanding of tanks and tank warfare. New to tanks and the Tank Corps, Patton had quickly learned all that was to be learned about tanks. This report is arguably the most important paper ever written by Patton and laid the groundwork for the United States Tank Corps.

Consisting essentially of four sections, the paper dealt with the mechanical structure of the tank, the organization of tank units, the tactics of tank forces, and methods of instruction and drill. In the first section, Patton described the tank as an armored vehicle whose main goal was to deliver power on the battlefield as required. Patton submitted that in order for this to happen, the tank must follow three principles:

1st. It must be able to overcome all the obstacles incident to the terrain.
2d. It must be able to give a maximum protection to its operatives and its motor power.
3d. It must be armed.[58]

Patton understood that mobility and firepower, not sheer mass and size, were key to armored warfare. Through mobility the tank could attack quickly, but more important, with increased speed and quickness the tank would face less fire and be less vulnerable to enemy attacks.

This first section of the paper is impressive for enumerating all the deficiencies Patton discovered at the Renault factory he visited in December 1917. Patton wrote out in exacting detail twenty-six changes that United States manufactures should incorporate. He noted that the French Renault factory continued "to make tanks containing faults to which . . . attention has been drawn by the people using them at Champlieu, while on the other hand the people at Champlieu fail to remonstrate with sufficient vehemence and continue to accept imperfect materiel."[59] Patton was focused on ensuring that the American manufactures would heed his advice. One of the changes Patton recommended was a better self-starter. "The inside system of cranking is very efficient so long as the tank is in a level position," he wrote, "but when a tank is stalled at a steep angle it is almost impossible to crank it from the inside."[60] Americans being larger and taller than their European counterparts, Patton recommended that American manufactures build tanks with eye slots for both the driver and gunner raised one and a half inches higher than in the European-built tanks.[61] He recommended a speaking tube between the driver and gunner, a Rolls-Royce-type fan belt for added durability, helmets for tankers, and even different wing nuts for the gearbox.[62] Many of these recommendations would be added or adopted later in 1918 and for the American-built tanks.

Section B of the paper deals with organizing tank forces. Patton believed a platoon should consist of 1 tank with a three-inch gun, 2 tanks with six-pound guns, and 2 tanks with machine guns, giving a platoon a total of 5 tanks and 15 men. A company should then consist of three platoons and a company headquarters. Overall, a company should consist of 5 officers, 96 men, 25 tanks, and 12 vehicles. Next came the formation of a battalion, which in Patton's conception consisted of three companies plus a battalion headquarters and a repair depot. The battalion would need 18 officers, 331 men, 77 tanks, and 42 vehicles.[63]

Section C of the paper deals with tactics and training. While a firm believer in tanks, Patton, unlike J. F. C. Fuller, saw the tank as an aid for the infantry. Thus the main tactical purposes of a tank were to assist the infantry's advance by running over wire, prevent the enemy from manning trench defenses, shield the infantry from enemy machine-gun fire, help neutralize enemy strongholds with fire, patrol the field to prevent counterattacks, and finally, in true Patton form, to seize the initiative and attack beyond the final objective.[64] Also, while most tanks in World War I were inserted piecemeal, Patton correctly argued that for tanks to be effective, they must be massed and supported with infantry. Depth for tanks was just as important as ammunition for infantry.

In this section, as he would do throughout the war, Patton took time to denigrate the British and their tank corps. A lifelong Francophile, Patton believed the British had sabotaged the early tank work done by the French:

> The first use of the English tanks showed their possibilities and the French were forced to alter their carrying machines into attack machines. This adaption, however, was wholly unsatisfactory as the French tank had not sufficient power or climbing ability. Still, they had built so many that they could not make a new model without first giving the old revamped ones a trial. But the comparative inefficiency of their first tanks was shortly

proved by battle and they decided to construct a new machine purely for fighting purposes. To this end they started the manufacture of the Renault light tank but so far have made less than fifty. They expect, however, to have a large number in the spring of 1918.[65]

He did hold the two original French tanks, the fifteen-ton Schneider and the heavier, twenty-three-ton St. Chamond, in contempt, writing: "Neither of these tanks can progress without the aid of infantry accompaniment whose duty is to prepare for them crossings over trenches, and both of them are underpowered for work among shell holes."[66]

Long a reader and respecter of history, Patton wrote on the history of tanks in the war and analyzed their successes and failures during World War I. He quickly covered early successes and failures of the Allies at Jovincourt and Laffoux in 1917. Patton correctly devoted considerable attention to the Battle of Cambrai and the British failure to understand the strengths and weaknesses of their tanks:

At Cambrai during the period from November 27 to December 1, 1917, the British attacked with 432 tanks in two echelons, 332 in the first echelon and a reserve of 100 tanks. . . . In the sixteen days of artillery preparation and counter-barrage preceding the battle of Ypres the infantry had ten thousand casualties before the zero hour. At Cambrai there were none. After the zero hour on the first day at Cambrai the loss[, out] of seventy-five thousand men engaged[,] was only some three hundred, much lower than usual. The percentage of killed to hit was also much lower than usual, owing to the fact that practically all the wounds were from rifle bullets instead of shell fragments. The loss of tanks on the first day they were used in the offensive was only ten per cent. Up to December 1st their loss was twenty-five per cent, men and tanks, but this was due to the fact that strong counter attacks made it necessary to use them on the defensive where being limited in movement the hostile artillery found their range with disastrous results . . . Wherever the tanks went the infantry met with success, except where the tanks got ahead of the infantry. . . . Had the heavy British tanks been followed by an equal number of light tanks to mop up after them and to push past them and exploit their success better results would undoubtedly have been obtained.[67]

The last section of the paper deals mainly with theory, and Patton emphasizes again that tanks are designed and equipped to support the infantry. He argues that tanks and their crew must do six things in coordination with the infantry:

1) They must precede the infantry at the zero hour.
2) They must prevent hostile infantry from manning the parapet when the barrage lifts.
3) They must prevent machine guns and trench cannon from attacking the infantry.
4) They must help in the mopping up and must neutralize the resistance of strong points and blockhouses by masking them with fire and smoke bombs. To do this they must remain in the first position until the infantry has gained secure possession. The history of tank action shows that wherever the tanks have gone ahead before the infantry were in full possession it had invariably resulted in loss to the latter.
5) They must guard against counter-attack.
6) When the final objective has been consolidated they must push on at their own initiative and seek every opportunity to become pursuit cavalry.[68]

Patton also argued that there was no need for tank echelons above the brigade level and wanted to focus on the Tank Centers as the administrative headquarters of the Tank Corps.[69] As regards light tanks, he correctly wrote, "Mobility is a most essential feature in all arms and is the chief place where the light tank has an advantage over the heavy."[70] Lastly, he warned that the "worst enemy of the tank is the small cannon firing directly at short range. For this purpose the Germans use the 37-millimeter and 77-millimeter on a low mount. Another enemy is very wide ditches which have not been shattered by shell fire."[71] While this was written in the theory section of the paper, it is true that most of the American losses to tank crews and equipment were from German artillery fire and enemy trenches.

At the end of the report, Patton wrote in the margins: "This paper was and is the basis of the US Tank Corps I think it is the best technical paper I ever wrote."[72] He was right. While Patton had a tendency to misspell words, his official work is well written both for clarity and depth. He was new to tanks and the Tank Corps, but his report would have been a notable achievement for any officer, regardless of rank. For such a young and junior officer to write such a precise report shows the ability and potential of Patton as a future commander and leader. This report was written in an era when the United States Army had almost no specialty or support branches—what it now calls "functional areas." Functional area officers are typically drawn from more traditional military branches and train on very specific tasks. Generally, these officers remove themselves from potential promotions and higher commands, but they are vital to how a modern army fights. In 1917 these officers and other specialty branches did not exist. With the growth of functional areas and specialty branches, there is little chance in today's army that an officer in Patton's position would be able to write any part of such a report, and the technical aspects of the paper would likely be written by more senior and experienced officers, along with countless staff and support personnel.

Patton must have realized the success of the report, as he wrote to his wife after submitting it: "Honestly I think not many men could have combined the exact mechanical knowledge with the general Tactical and organization knowledge to do it. But I think I did a good job in fact I surprised my self and hope others will think as well of it as I do."[73]

On 15 December, Patton left Pershing's staff and was now in charge of building the United States Tank Corps. But first he needed land, soldiers, and tanks. As he left his relatively safe staff position, Patton wrote to his wife explaining his reasons for leaving Pershing's side:

I have always talked blood and murder and am looked on as an advocate of close up fighting. I could never look my self in the face if I was a staff officer and comparatively safe. The men who get on the staffs now will stay on them and see other men from the line pass and beat them. The Tanks were I truly believe a great opportunity for me I ought to be one of the high ranking men one of the two or three at top. I am fitted for it as I have imagination and daring and exceptional mechanical knowledge. I believe Tanks will be much more important than aviation and the man on the ground floor will reap the benefit.[74]

3

The Tank Master

Patton and the Tank Center

(15 December 1917–20 August 1918)

> I have got nineteen officers here now and will have the first two
> companies of men as soon as I get the French to give me the
> land.
>
> —Patton to Beatrice Patton, 17 January 1918

Patton, after transferring to the United States Tank Corps, was now the head of the first light tank school in the nation's history. He had yet to develop the reputation for training he would attain by 1938 and would show in the lead-up to American entry into World War II. In many ways this position was the most important in Patton's life. How he performed would make or break his career. Patton understood this. To be director of the Light Tank School, while not a command position technically, was a key developmental position, something that was just as vital for American officers a century ago as it is today. For many officers then and now, careers are defined by these pivotal positions.

For training, Patton wanted all the officers and noncommissioned officers and as many soldiers as possible to complete a four-week course, after which they would instruct new arrivals. After the training of two full companies, these companies would instruct anywhere from two to four new companies, so that after three months Patton hoped to have two battalions trained.[1] The most important of Patton's training ideas was that the training instructors would be the future unit commanders. For soldiers, the only requirement Patton made was that they have mechanical experience, meaning some familiarity with automobiles and/or engines. While Patton's training concepts worked fairly well, the school was almost constantly faced with a tank shortage, and this hindered his job effectiveness and the soldiers' training more than anything else.

Finding the land on which to train soldiers proved to be harder than it would seem. For the training center Patton chose Bourg, a small village in northeast France five miles south of Langres, where the US Army schools were concentrated.[2] The ground was level and perfect for tank training, and a lone railroad track would be beneficial in getting troops and eventually tanks to the center. As Patton and others realized already, tanks could not operate without close rail support. If forced to drive more than a short distance, World War I tanks tended to break down for a variety of reasons, one of the biggest being issues with fan belts. At first the French refused to allow the Americans access to the land. This infuriated Patton, who was beginning to feel that the French were acting more like enemies than allies. "We are more or less held up now by the French who seem to put every obstacle in the way of our getting the ground we want for Tank center. I am going down in a few minutes to see the French Mission and see what I can do. You would think they were doing us a great favor to let us fight in their damn country."[3]

Much as he had during the past summer when he tried to get his wife overseas, Patton became depressed, this time over the slow progress of establishing the tank school, the difficulty in acquiring the land, and a general feeling of not getting the job done. By January 1918, Patton was writing dreary letters to his wife about his mental state. "I am feeling very low over the Tanks again to day. Every thing seems to be getting in the way and no one can tell when we will ever get any tanks. I am disgusted with the whole business."[4] His mood was at least buoyed by his promotion chances. By the end of the month he was only eleven spots away from being promoted to major.[5] For such a rank-driven officer, Patton was not as elated as one would think. He understood that any promotion to major and beyond would be only temporary and he would return to his permanent rank of captain once the war was over.

While his wife received letters about Patton's depression, his soldiers felt his wrath in person. Without land and tanks, Patton focused on discipline and was already gaining a reputation for his hardened approach to discipline and training. The lack of tanks just made his reputation grow:

Unless I get some Tanks soon I will go crazy for I have done nothing of any use since November and it is getting on my nerves. I cussed a reserve officer for saluting me with his hands in his pockets to day and he said that he demanded to be treated like an officer. I almost hit him but compromised by taking him to

the General who cussed him good. Some of these new officers
are the end of the limit. I bet the Tank Corps will have discipline
if nothing else.[6]

By the end of January 1918, the Tank School and the infant United
States Tank Corps were beginning to grow. Patton had shown himself to
be a good administrator and staff officer so far, but now it was time to
see how Patton was as a trainer of tankers.

In preparation for establishing and running a tank school, Patton
had time to write "Memorandum No. 1." This first memo to the Tank
School was typical of the beliefs and behaviors Patton had developed
on Pershing's staff both in Mexico and in France, and it echoed an earlier memo he had written in December 1917. There Patton wrote that
"all members of the Tank Service shall be models in respect to soldierly
appearance and deportment."[7] In World War II, Patton would be labeled
a martinet and overly preoccupied with appearance; as commander of
the Tank School, Patton was no different, decreeing, "Officers and men
will shave daily and will see that their hair is kept short. Not clipped but
kept short so that they look like soldiers and not like poets."[8] Patton
wrote later to his wife about his reputation within the growing tank center, "I am getting a hell of a reputation for a skunk when officers don't
salute me I stop them and make them do it. I also reported a reserve
lieutenant to day for profanity. I expect some of them would like to poi-
son me I will have to eat eggs like Louis XI."[9] A few days later Patton
would file his first charges, against an officer who accidentally lost secret
papers. Patton remarked about the situation, "He is only a kid so I am
sorry for him but one can't run a war on sentiment."[10] To Patton, war
was serious business, and he had to handle his men as sternly as possible. The incident does show that Patton had a personal side and cared
for his soldiers, and like Pershing, his great role model, he did not suffer fools gladly. Now as a tank director he had the power to end careers,
and while he did not relish the duty, it was a duty he would fulfill time
and time again in both world wars.

Without tanks or land, Patton made sure his soldiers still received
small-arms and small-unit training. On 30 January his mood suddenly
changed. This day was an important day for Patton, the Light Tank
School, and the growing United States Tank Corps, as the French agreed
to sell land to the American Expeditionary Force. Perhaps more important, Patton and Rockenbach decided to send Lieutenant Elgin Braine
back to the United States to lead the army's effort to build Renault tanks.

Braine, who helped Patton write his initial tank report, was an indispensible figure to Patton and the establishment of the Tank Corps. Now he was asked to help coordinate the planning and building of American tanks with factories and businesses across the United States. It is important to note that Braine was only a first lieutenant and entrusted with arguably one of the most complex and messy tasks ever issued in the United States Army. Ultimately Braine's hard work would not pay off, as no American tanks would reach France before the end of the war. However, that was not the fault of a young and brilliant officer like Braine, but of the massively growing and uncontrolled bureaucracy of the United States government and the tone-deaf and overly greedy industrial companies paid to produce the tanks. On 31 January, Patton wrote in his diary about Braine, "Lt. Braine left for Paris to day. I was sorry to see him go he is the most reliable man I have yet met and had plenty of sense."[11] Braine played a pivotal and major role in World War I and the creation of the United States Tank Corps, but he would spend the rest of the war traveling across the United States by rail in a doomed attempt to get the United States War Department and giant companies to agree on plans and prices to produce American tanks.

While Patton was sad to see Braine leave, it was an important and necessary mission. The United States Tank Corps consisted mainly of Rockenbach and Patton and a few other soldiers by the end of January. This was also the first time Patton wrote to his family and in his diary about his relationship with Rockenbach. Patton would never develop a lasting friendship or relationship with Rockenbach—the two were just very different—but they did balance each other, and Patton maintained enough of a relationship with his commander because he understood that success and promotions rested with Rockenbach:

Col. R. is the most contrary old cuss I ever worked with as soon as you suggest any thing he opposed but after about an hours argument comes round and proposed the same thing him self. So in the long run I get my way, but at a great waste of breath. It is good discipline however for me for I have to keep my temper. At the end of each argument I feel completely done up. I guess he does too. Still he is trying to have me made a Lieutenant Colonel so I ought not be too hard on him.[12]

In Rockenbach's defense, Patton never fully grasped how much the Tank Corps chief helped his career and reduced bureaucratic entanglements on Patton and the Tank School that would likely have depressed Patton even more.

As action reports about the Battle of Cambrai began to hit the newspapers, for the first time tanks were the talk of Paris and the entire Western Front. The battle was not considered a defeat, nor a success, and the degree to which the tanks performed varied widely. Patton, however, believed the battle showed the potential of the tank, writing, "It is a big job and I feel sure that tanks in some form will play a part in all future wars. They are in idea simply a heavy armored infantry soldier at least that is the theory of operation of the light tanks. The heavy are a little different. My fear is that the fighting will be over before we get any or enough for it too few they will not ackomplish their mission."[13]

By the start of February, Patton officially had the Light Tank School up and running. On 1 February he held what he recorded in his diary as the "first Tank drill in history of U. S. Army."[14] Furthermore, he was reassured by both Rockenbach and the French that Renault tanks would be arriving by the middle of March.[15] With more than two hundred men, and finally established in Bourg, Patton provided the best environment for his troops that he could give. Though a strong disciplinarian who could come off as uncaring, Patton did care for his soldiers and tried his best to make sure they were comfortable. To not care would be a dereliction of duty, and Patton was constantly fighting for better conditions for his soldiers.

Busy around the clock, a typical day for soldiers in the Tank School began at 6:30 a.m. with company close-order drills, saluting, and issues of exactness. From 8:55 to 9:25, the soldiers worked out, ran, and performed light calisthenics, or what the current United States soldier would call PT, physical training. From 9:30 to 10:20, soldiers would practice signal drills at the platoon level, followed by a quick ten-minute exercise in guard duty and military courtesy. At 10:45, soldiers would train in their companies, working on close company drills, foot drills, and other military drills. After a lunch break, usually from 11:30 to 1:00 p.m., officers would drill and practice pistol shooting and instruction, generally led by Patton himself. From 1:50 to 2:30, all officers trained and worked on drills, lectures, and extra duties. After that the last class, from 2:50 to 4:00, was on gas engines and learning how to drive and maintain a tank.[16] Lieutenant Julian K. Morrison best summed up the experience at Bourg under Patton.

Looking back now over the months spent in training at the old Tank School at Bourg, France, the writer can recall many pleasant ones interspersed with long days of tedious study. It's a working organization, this Tank Corps, and were it not for the indomitable spirit of its members and the ability not only to make the best of things, but to find pleasure in their work there might have been a number of A.W.O.L.'s not only among the enlisted men but of officers as well. Every day, some Sunday's excepted, a fixed schedule was carried out from daylight to dark and then for the officer's school at night. The writer always got a great deal of encouragement from these lectures, usually given by Colonel Patton. He was made to understand by the Colonel that a tank officer was meant to die. His favorite message to his officers was "Go forward, go forward. If your tank breaks down go forward with the Infantry. There will be no excuse for your failure in this, and if I find any tank officer behind the Infantry I will—." All tank officers know the rest.[17]

While at the Tank School, Patton was well respected but also feared. His fierceness led soldiers to label the Tank Corps the Suicide Club.[18] Patton likely was more than receptive to the name!

Patton remained fixated on discipline. As he had shown as a staff officer earlier in the war, he demanded exactness and correctness and repeated these lessons over and over again to his officers and senior enlisted soldiers. Throughout the war he constantly lectured his soldiers on discipline. Patton, like many officers before him and since, used football as an analogy. He enjoyed the sport and had wanted to play while attending West Point. He had the size, but unlike Dwight Eisenhower, who was a rising star on the team before injuries ended his football career, Patton was not a good player, nor particularly athletic. In a specific lecture given to his soldiers, he wrote: "Discipline instant, cheerful, unhesitating and automatic obedience" and compared it to a quarterback calling a play in a huddle. The rest of the team had to instantly and automatically follow the play or else the play would fail and the team would lose. He added that he did not enjoy discussing discipline as often as he did and did not like correcting officers on a daily basis, but said it was "our mutual duty to each other and to our country which forces us to make these corrections." Lastly, he reinforced the notion that without discipline, armies and nations lose wars, and again portrayed war as a great sporting contest, telling his soldiers: "Lack of discipline in war means death or defeat. The prize for a game is nothing. The prize for this war is the greatest of all prizes—Freedom."[19] Certainly Patton was prone to hyperbole, especially in talks or lectures with his soldiers, but this was not atypical of Patton or of officers both then and now. Discipline is a fundamental hallmark of great armies, and Patton was going to do everything in his power to make his unit disciplined.

With the Tank School up and running, Patton wrote another paper, this one titled "Tank Drill and Training Manual." Like his lecture on discipline it is perhaps over the top, but it offers the reader great insight into the leadership ability and initiative of Patton. "Success in battle presupposes the destruction of the enemy. This is brought about by killing and wounding his men so as to reduce his strength and destroy his morale. The above happy results may only be looked for when the training has been intelligent and thorough, so that the men are educated in what to do and have the discipline to do it."[20]

Along these lines of training and discipline Patton molded his very green soldiers into professional and efficient warriors. Patton's decision to move to tanks was paying off, and on 17 February he received news that he had been promoted to the rank of major, effective 15 December 1917. Though he had not received official guidance, Patton decided it was safe to pin on the gold oak leaves of a major, writing to his wife: "I was promoted Major on Dec 15. I have not heard officially yet but after much debated I decided to put on my leaves and now I am wearing them. I feel sort of like a thief but that does not bother me at all as there are so many militia majors around here that one must have leaves to keep ones self respect." Patton ended the letter with a joke, telling his wife, "Inspite of my increased rank I still love you."[21] Little did Patton know, he was going to be promoted again in less than a month.

During this time Patton's mood clearly grew more positive, as he had more work to do and it was work he believed was valuable. He did, however, as always, have time to write to his wife. Generally, despite his colorful language and stern attitude with his men, Patton's letters to his wife were fairly family focused and censored. He sometimes joked about their long separation. In a rare letter written in February 1918, he wrote about their eventual reunion: "When this war is over I am going to insist on using a single bed for *both* of us at the same time. There is perhaps more than one reason for this, but the only one which the censor and modesty will allow me to mention is that I am tired of being cold and especially of getting into a large and empty bed full of cold sheets. Hence you will have to go to bed first."[22]

In March, Patton along with General Rockenbach spent a week in England, and Patton attempted to get some modifications for his tanks.

"I argued in favor of four speeds, but was ruled an ass."[23] Patton once again showed his evolving intellect, as he correctly asserted that mobility, not armor or more guns, was the key to tanks being successful in the Great War. Following the trip, Rockenbach conducted his first inspection of the Tank School and was extremely impressed. Patton made little mention of it, but no doubt it was more evidence that he had made the correct decision in joining the United States Tank Corps. His decision would look even sweeter by mid-March.

On March 19, Patton received word that he was promoted to lieutenant colonel. Throughout the war, he often learned of his promotions in letters from his wife or through rumor and hearsay. It was in a letter from Beatrice that he found out about this one. "I just got your wire address to Lt. Col. Patton it is the first I had heard of it but I hope you are right. . . . I am not so hellish young and it is not spring yet still I love you just as much as if we were twenty two on the baseball grand stand at W[est] P[oint] the night I graduated." Patton, however, showed mild modesty with his promotion to lieutenant colonel. Without the war, he would likely not have made lieutenant colonel for another fifteen to twenty years, and it is possible he would never have been promoted to that rank at all. He understood his luck and added, "If I am a Lt. Col. I have surely done something and feel like an imposter though dangerous modesty is not one of my many faults." As he had done earlier in his deployment to Europe, Patton ended his letter to his wife with a gentle reminder to "die your hair if necessary as I don't like gray haired people."[24]

The good news kept coming for the new lieutenant colonel as he received word that ten Renault tanks were en route to the growing tank school. However, his euphoria was punctured when on 21 March 1918 he received word that Frederick Ayer, his father-in-law, had passed away. Patton was extremely close to both his wife's parents, but he was especially fond of her father. Patton wrote in his diary that "our Commander has gone has gone from us."[25] While Patton could be cruel and detached emotionally from his family at times, his letters to his wife display his extreme care for her and her family:

Darling one I know what the death of your father must mean to you but you ought to take great very great comfort in the fact that most of his pleasure in the last years of his life were due to you and your beautiful and unselfish love for him. . . . It is a great source of pleasure and pride to me that Mr. Ayer who is the most perfect mortal I know of took an interest and a pride in my present work, and his last letter to me will ever be an inspiration to me in this or any other work. . . . I know Darling that you are suffering all that the human soul can suffer but hope that the spirit of your father will help and support you in the hours now passing.[26]

Though saddened by the loss of his father-in-law, Patton was extremely happy to finally receive ten Renaults on March 23. Once the trains arrived with the tanks, it fell to Patton to unload the tanks and get them to the school. The problem was that Patton was the only American who had ever driven a tank. Despite the French saying it would take more than fifteen hours to unload the tanks, Patton bragged that he did it in three hours. "No one but me had ever driven one so I had to back them all off the train but then I put some men on them and they went along all right. I took one through some heavy woods this morning and it just ate up the brush like nothing. Tomorrow they will all be oiled up and we will start active business making drivers on Tuesday. It will be fine having something to work with."[27]

The ten tanks having arrived at night, Patton backed seven of them out in short order, and the tanks were slowly driven back to the Tank School. Patton was especially proud of the troops. "This shows the adaptability of the American Soldier, for totally inexperienced as they were, they drove the tanks by night . . . over two kilometers and landed them without accident at the designated point."[28]

As the tanks arrived, Patton was elated to put his first "Gold V" on his left sleeve signifying he had been in a combat zone for six months. Never happy with what he had, Patton remarked rather naively, "If we get wounded we wear the same on the right arm for each wound. I would like to be hit in some nice fat part so I could get one."[29] With new rank and new awards, Patton was busy training and building his tank school and readying his troops for combat. Despite all the work, Patton still managed to write regularly and drew up another memo for the United States Tank Corps. In this undated memo written sometime in March 1918, Patton correctly insisted that the trainers and instructors train the troops they would ultimately lead into battle and urged them that "this is a principle which must never be departed from." Proving to be just as excellent a trainer as he was a staff officer, Patton wrote in the memo: "Efficient instructers and leaders are essential indifferent ones must be ruthlessly weeded out. Officers must not content themselves with the teaching and knowledge they gain, but they must supplement these by personal study and effort."[30]

Just as the Tank School was beginning to show progress, Patton received more sad news from his family. Following the death of his father-in-law, his mother-in-law, seemingly in good health, passed away just a few weeks later. On 10 April, Patton once again had to write to his wife about the loss of a parent: "I got the telegram about your mother on the 9th Last night after the mail had closed. . . . It seems heartless thing to say but I think that Ellie is happier than she would have been to have continued on with out your father. They were as nearly one as is possible to be—as nearly one as we are. . . . I do not think I would care much about keeping on if you were gone."[31]

Once again Patton had to try his best to be a loving husband despite being overseas and training for combat. Patton had been, and continued to be, concerned about his wife. In the spring of 1918, while still relatively young and in good shape, Beatrice Patton had struggled on and off with her health during her husband's time in Mexico and in France. While Beatrice would prove to her husband and her family that she was tough enough to handle Patton's long absences, during the war she was desperate for another child. Their third child, however, would have to wait until after the war ended.[32]

Following a few weeks of training with actual tanks, Patton and his troops put on their first tank demonstration. The 22 April demonstration went extremely well, and Patton was pleased. "The show came off all right except that it was raining hard and very cold so that one got stuck in a shell hole but I had a reserve one ready and every thing went on fine." He also noted that the "only accidences occurred in the case of a general staff officers who fell off their horses. . . . Six fell off."[33]

To celebrate the Tank School's success and show the maturity of the Tank Corps, six days later Patton organized the first light tank battalion. His three company commanders were Captains Earnest Herman, Joseph W. Viner, and Sereno E. Brett, and Patton was of course the battalion commander.[34] Brett, who would develop into Patton's right-hand man following the departure of Lieutenant Braine, became one of the most important figures in the early days of the United States Tank Corps and was one of the few to stay with the tanks after the 1920 National Defense Act ended the independent Tank Corps. Patton had pushed hard to get Brett transferred into the Tank Corps. Prior to joining Patton, Brett was a lead instructor on the 37-millimeter machine gun and had impressed Patton early on during the arrival of more officers in France. His selection of Brett was one of Patton's best decisions of World War I.

While extremely happy with the progress of his soldiers and the Tank School itself, Patton had grown bored with the safety of rear duty and longed for a glimpse of the front. "I am getting ashamed of my self when I think of all the fine fighting and how little I have had to do with it," he wrote, then, mentioning someone who was recently wounded in the fleshy part of the leg, he added, "I rather envie him as now he can wear a wound chevron and pose as a hero."[35] On May 21, Patton finally had a chance to travel to the front. Eager to see the front, yet apprehensive, Patton wrote his father the day he left: "I am leaving in a few moments for the French front to go with a bunch of french tanks. I am hoping that the Bosch will start something but the prospects are not good and besides I have too much rank to see any thing. . . . I left a box containing my dress uniforms and some other things at a fencing room . . . I have told Viner about it and he will send them to B. if any thing happens. As I said before nothing will."[36]

During his two weeks at the front, Patton had one experience of note. Traveling with a French major named La Favre, Patton got within two hundred yards of the German line. Unafraid and willing to trade his life for a bit of fun, La Favre turned toward the German line and exposed his bottom to enemy fire as he adjusted his leggings. Patton, amazed but not to be outdone, took off his helmet, lit a cigarette, and began to smoke. Luckily for both La Favre and Patton, German sharpshooters decided not to fire on the show-offs.[37] Patton commented to his wife, "It was about the same thrill as riding a steeplechase."[38] For Patton this behavior was not uncommon, but it is hard to take his thoughts about combat as more bluster than honesty. To calm his wife, Patton took a piece of shell that exploded near him on the trip and had it made into a bracelet; he hoped that she would like it, since "it might have made you a widow."[39]

Returning from his rather adventurous trip in June, Patton reorganized the Tank School and formed a second battalion, giving him command of two battalions. Becoming the equivalent of a modern-day brigade commander, Patton appointed a chief of staff, an adjutant, a reconnaissance officer, and a supply officer. He placed Captain Viner in command of the first battalion, designated the 326th Tank Battalion, and Captain Brett in command of the second battalion, designated the 327th Tank Battalion.[40] Under Viner's command there were three companies: Company A led by Captain Ranulf Compton, Company B led by Lieutenant Newell P. Weed, and Company C under the command of Captain Math L. English. All three of these company commanders would perform admirably under Patton's command, with Compton eventually taking over Brett's battalion. Under Brett's command—and Patton viewed Brett as his best commander—there were four companies, Company A under Captain Harry H. Semmes, Company B under First Lieutenant William H. Williams, Company C under Captain Courtney H. Barnard, and under Lieutenant Ellis Baldwin the 301st Repair and Salvage Company, which would prove to be essential to keeping Patton's tanks in service.[41] It is important to note that the battalions were originally designated the 326th and 327th. The units maintained these number designations until the Meuse-Argonne offensive. Just as that operation started, the 326th Tank Battalion became the 344th and the 327th Tank Battalion the 345th.[42] The 1st Tank Brigade, which Patton commanded directly, was also redesignated the 304th Tank Brigade.[43]

With two battalions in order, Patton began a paper titled "Brief Notes on the Tactical Employment of Tanks." Once again showing his evolution in thinking, he wrote on some themes that would carry over into World War II: "It must never be forgotten that boldness is the key to victory. The tank must be used boldly. It is new and always has the element of surprise. It is also very terrifying to look at as the infantry soldier is helpless before it."[44]

By June, Patton thought the Tank School was in good enough order that he accepted a spot in the Army General Staff College in Langres. While busy with the Tank School and not really interested in staff duty, Patton decided to take the class because most general officers had taken it. Also, during the class Patton met with and got to know numerous officers who would play important roles in World War II. Among them were Major Adna R. Chaffee, who would become the staunchest tank advocate between the wars, Lieutenant Colonel George C. Marshall, who served as army chief of staff during World War II and was perhaps the most important military officer in modern United States history, Major William H. Simpson, who commanded the Ninth Army, Captain Joseph Stilwell, who led United States forces in China and Burma, and Captain John S. Wood, commander of the 4th Armored Division, who would later serve under Patton in the Third Army and was arguably the most brilliant of America's tank commanders.[45]

In between Staff College, training, and running the Tank School, Patton wrote a long and extensive lecture to the General Staff School that he presented on 22 July 1918. Like his earlier tank report, Patton's lecture is remarkably clear, presenting the basic premise of tanks, the training center, and how tanks would interact with other branches in the United States Army. The lecture was a major achievement for Patton. Not only would he lecture to faculty and fellow officers, but he was afforded an early opportunity to get his fellow officers to understand the strengths and weaknesses of the tank.

The first page of the lecture outlined the organization of the Tank Corps and the Tank School: "The largest unit of the U. S. Tank Corps is the Tank Center, the appropriate complement for an A.C. A Center consists of 4 battalions, 1 of heavy machines and 3 of light. In the heavy battalion there are 3 companies of 15 fighting machines each, each company arranged in 5 3-tank platoons, or 15 platoons for the battalion."[46] Following this bare-bones look at how the Tank Corps was organized, Patton laid out for the audience six principles of tank warfare that he would adhere to for the war and the succeding interwar years. Patton argued that tanks and their crews must do these six things in order to be successful and help the United States Army win the war:

1. They must help keep down the hostile infantry and prevent its manning the fire trench.
2. They must cut the wire.
3. They must help put out machine gun nests.
4. They must help mop up.
5. They must help repel counter attacks.
6. They must help to exploit the success and get into the first hostile gun positions, then either putting out the gun crews, or at least diverting their fire to themselves and away from the infantry.[47]

Patton, like Rockenbach, showed political astuteness, and the two expressed their views carefully in public. Both men understood that many American officers, especially infantry officers, did not view tanks favorably, or at best were skeptical of their chances. Patton was very deliberate in public to tie tanks to the infantry. He did this for two reasons.

First, he did not want to gain a reputation as a specialist or tank zealot. Doing so, Patton feared, would limit his chances for promotion following the end of the war. He had expressed this fear to his father, and to his wife earlier in the year when he wrote, "As to my staying Tanks after the war I doubt it because it is a specialty. And specialists don't get supreme command. Besides we will have another war in Mexico and Tanks would be useless there so I will be back in the Cavalry. At least that is my present notion."[48] While it is likely Patton was more conflicted in this decision, he never expressed another opinion on the matter, and by 1920 he would return to his original commissioning branch, the cavalry.

The other reason Patton wanted to tie tanks to the infantry was that light tanks had little chance of success without infantry support. Patton later in the lecture wrote, "The infantry win the fights, the tanks only and always help the infantry to win them. Any other theory of using tanks is utterly wrong."[49] Patton's views on effective tank tactics and the importance of the interaction with the infantry were correct for 1918. The Renault tank, while much more capable than the heavier British and French tanks, was not yet capable of independent operation. Without infantry support, the tanks were not going to be able to sustain the offensive, and they were of little use in defensive operations. Yet even as he tempered his belief about the future of the tank publicly, Patton still pushed for aggressive and offensive actions.

Patton's numerous lectures, letters, memos, and written notes during the war should be viewed as an information operation. Patton understood correctly that as director of the first American tank center he had a responsibility not only to train tankers for the war but to sell the rest of the United States Army on the armored innovation. During this era when the United States Army was still skeptical of the tank, it was left to Patton to persuade the rest of the officer corps of the potential and applicability of the tank in modern war. While he proved to be a very effective trainer, his salesmanship of the tank and the United States Tank Corps was less successful. This is not a criticism of Patton, as he would convince division and corps commanders later in the war about the viability of the tank, but he had a nearly impossible task, and the United States Army of World War I was still focused on more traditional branches such as artillery and infantry.

Patton was relatively happy with his lecture and wrote to his wife, "I have undoubtedly inherited Pa's 'gift of gab.' I gave a lecture to the Line School to day and five or six officers told me it was the best lecture they had ever heard over here and one said it was the best lecture he had ever heard by a soldier or civilian."[50] Whether those officers were being polite or not is lost to history, but it was apparent that Patton was becoming known throughout the United States Army as a competent lecturer and the leading theorist on tanks and tank warfare. Not all were as impressed with Patton's growing "gift of gab" as Patton was with himself. After the war, on 20 February 1919, Patton's father wrote a remarkable and scathing letter to his son:

Among other things I have been worrying for fear that the "gift of gab" you have developed may get you trouble—unless restrained such a gift is always dangerous the temptation to say smart or striking things is hard to resist—and it is only next day—that cold reason condemns. You are now 34—and a Col and the dignity going with your rank invests that you say with more importance so I hope in your speeches you will be very careful & self restrained—for your own good & our future— Another gift you have developed I really regret—and that is the ability to write verse upon vulgar & smutty subjects. That is very dangerous. The very men to whom you read & recite such stuff as your last one will laugh—and apparently enjoy—but you have really lowered yourself in their eyes—above all it lacks *dignity*— and you need to cultivate that especially in view of your rank. . . . All the really big men I have known—abstained from repeating vulgar stories—and all who were facile in speech—cultivated great reserve—or if they sometimes forgot themselves—always suffered for the lapse.[51]

This letter must have rocked Patton and caused him to reflect on his service in the war, but as his firing at the end of World War II would show, it seemed Patton did not take the advice of his father, or if he did, it was long forgotten by 1945.

In addition to writing lectures, attending classes, and running the tank school, Patton attempted to get approval from the American Expeditionary Force for new tank tactics. The tactics were not revolutionary, but his suggestions were quickly shot down by Lieutenant Colonel D. D. Pullen, who wrote to Patton on 25 July:

While I believe that your proposed tactics are sound, I do not think this is the time to propose any tactics for the Tank Corps. Our first job is to get Tanks and then the second job is to get some Tank fighting units in the line. After we get some Tank units up back of the line ready to take part in the fight we will be in position to talk about Tank tactics, and after we have been in one or more shows we will not only be in a position to talk Tank tactics, but we will be able to state exactly what we want and I believe what we say at that time will be accepted while at the present time a great deal of what we say will be looked upon as hot air.[52]

Pullen was correct here, and his reasoning was sound. Patton took the rejection well, but it was a sign that his theories on tanks and tank warfare were rapidly evolving and he was beginning to rock the status quo. Pullen, like Rockenbach, handled Patton's ideas with professionalism and maturity during the war. They were often able to tell Patton "no" but at the same time applaud Patton's effort and thinking. Even in World War I, it was becoming apparent to those that worked with Patton that he was a bold and energetic officer, but often he needed a more senior officer above him to check his "good ideas."

Serving double duty at the Tank Center and General Staff College, Patton was able to complete both tasks, and things were going smoothly. Finally, on 20 August 1918, Patton got his chance to prove that the United States Tank Corps was the best in the world. While in class, he received an urgent message that read: "You will report at once to the Chief of Tank Corps accompanied by your Reconnaissance officer and equipped for field service."[53] For Patton, this was the dream come true. For the first time in his life, he would lead men into battle.

4

Combat

St. Mihiel

(20 August–14 September 1918)

> The Tank Brigade Commander will remain at Corps H.Q. or be
> in close telephonic communication with it.
> —Samuel D. Rockenbach to Patton, 16 September 1918

In the late summer of 1918, the American Expeditionary Force had
grown enough in size and in structure to participate fully in the war.
Though American forces had been pushed into battle to stop the German
summer offensive, the St. Mihiel attack would be the first major engagement the American Expeditionary Force would participate in as a fully
organized and independent force.[1]

Located twenty miles south of Verdun, the town of St. Mihiel had
fallen into German hands in 1914 following the Battle of the Marne.
Since then the salient had become an issue of concern for France and her
Allies as the Germans still held on to 150 square miles of French terri-
tory.[2] The salient formed a triangle about twenty-four miles wide and
fourteen miles deep. According to historian Carlo D'Este, "It was the
ideal place to baptize by fire an untested American army and in the process eliminate a long-standing threat to Verdun."[3]

While the cutting of the salient was important, the real objective was
the ancient fortress of Metz. Only thirty miles beyond St. Mihiel, the stra-
tegically important city of Metz was the prize both the Allies and Pershing wanted. The original plan to attack St. Mihiel was not just to cut it
off. The plan called for fifteen American divisions,[4] together with four
French divisions, to attack the flanks of the salient, achieve an all-out
breakthrough, and advance.

Unfortunately, British and French fears caused a change in the plan.
On 30 August, Field Marshal Haig believed the Germans were in decline
and this was his chance to end the war before 1919. Supported by Mar-

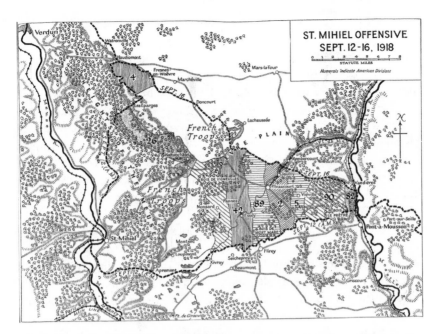

Source: St. Mihiel Offensive: (John J. Pershing, *My Experiences in the World War,* vol. 2 [New York: Stokes, 1931], 270).

shal Foch, Haig decided that a complete breakthrough of the St. Mihiel salient was risky and not worth the blood and expense. His new plan still called for the salient to be cut, but instead of pushing forward with an aggressive breakthrough, the forces were to free the railroad through St. Mihiel to Verdun and to establish a base for a major engagement against the Hindenburg Line.[5] This was a massive shaping operation to better prepare the Allies for the greater offensive operation to come. Following the cutting of the salient, the American Expeditionary Force would reorganize and swing north to the Meuse-Argonne portion of the Hindenburg Line.

With the final plan, Patton commenced to ready his Tank School and the 1st Tank Brigade. As he would later do in World War II, Patton set out to see the terrain on which his tanks would fight. During the last week of August, Patton and some French soldiers explored the section assigned to the tanks and the 1st Tank Brigade. Excited to once again visit the front, Patton was let down as "the Bosch whistled at us and we whistled back and having seen what we wanted went home."[6] Patton was even relaxed enough around the front to pick some daises that he sent home to his worried wife. While his letters to Beatrice seldom focused on death and the possibility of his being killed, Patton wrote a more serious note to his father and told him that if he was killed in action to "Please do what is best with any property I may have. Personally I hope you and mama keep it as Beatrice has plenty. I will send her my sword. I will give one horse to Gen. Pershing and one to Maj. Viner."[7] After Patton had returned from reconnaissance, he wrote to his wife with more details of his mission and told her that he had "found some gas but not very much it feels just like the beginning of hay fever."[8] As for the terrain, Patton found the ground soft but decided it was suitable for tank use. With this knowledge in hand, he set about devising his own plan for his tanks.

The final plan called for Patton's 1st Tank Brigade to work in the American 4th Corps sector, which was located near the town of Toul. Under the Allied plan, the 4th Corps and the United States 1st Corps were expected to drive northward and meet the advancing United States 5th Corps.[9] More specifically, Patton and the 1st Tank Brigade would support the 1st and 42nd Divisions, which were located almost directly in the center of the 4th Corps. With the organization of the forces outlined, Patton organized his plan accordingly. As he would be directing the attack, he appointed Viner to command and direct the Tank School in Bourg and moved Brett to command the 326th Tank Battalion and Ranulf Compton to lead the 327th Tank Battalion.[10] Viner would prove to be a capable replacement for Patton as Tank School director once Patton took command of the brigade in the field. Patton made it clear that Viner's relief was not because of poor performance but "made as an acknowledgment of his efficient service, and not the reverse, as might appear to a casual observer."[11] Compton, while competent, was considered the weaker battalion commander of the two by Patton and would be outshone by Brett in the following months of the war. Patton would also, throughout the remainder of the war, give Brett and his force more responsibility and more important missions than Compton's battalion.

After Patton and his staff had laid the foundation of their attack for the 4th Corps, the decision was made to move the 1st Tank Brigade to the American 5th Corps. By 3 September all work with the 5th corps for the attack was finalized, but later in the day a change to the plan was ordered: "4:30 p.m., orders were received to cease operations with the 5th Corps and report at once to the C[ommanding].G[eneral]. 4th Corps, at Toul, for duty. This change was necessitated by the failure of the British to supply tanks to co-operate with the 4th Corps, and their absence had to be made good by the American tanks."[12]

When Patton met with the 4th Corps chief of staff, he found that the "front assigned to the tanks was all out of proportion to the number of tanks then available, as the original plans had been made on the assumption that this front would have been occupied by a larger number of British tanks. The front required to be covered was reduced, and an initial reconnaissance was made from the vicinity of Beaumont."[13] The ground was not ideal for tanks, but Patton believed if it did not rain, the tanks could complete their mission.[14]

Despite all the planning already completed for the 4th Corps, Patton had to start from scratch. On 9 September, following more reconnaissance work and planning, Patton issued 1st Tank Brigade Field Order No. 1, covering the planned attack and the role of his tanks. The memo outlined the major objective of the operation, which was for the First Army to reduce the St. Mihiel salient with two simultaneous attacks, one from the south with the 4th Corps and 1st Corps on the left, and one from the west where the 5th Corps would attack on the right.[15] The 4th Corps, which Patton's force was assigned to, had three divisions, the 89th, 42d, and 1st Infantry Divisions, aligned east to west, with the 3d Infantry Division held in reserve. Patton's two battalions were to follow the infantry into the first German trench. The goal of the tanks and their crews was to destroy the machine-gun nests in the first trench line. Once that objective was met, the tanks were to move toward Maizerais and rally at the Rupt de Mad. There they were to await engineers to get a bridge open. Then the tanks would move across in the direction of Lamarche and wait to cross the Madine.

More specifically, Patton split his brigade to fight with both the 42d Division and the 1st Division. The 327th Tank Battalion was assigned to the 42d Infantry Division and was located between the Bois de Remières and the west edge of the Bois de la Sonnard.[16] The 326th Tank Battalion was assigned to the United States 1st Infantry Division, located to the west of the Rupt de Mad.[17] In closing his order, Patton warned against ditching the tanks and ordered his men to "unditch" them and move forward.[18]

Once the battle began, Brett's forces on the left were to cross the Rupt de Mad and lead the infantry until they reached the village of Nonsard. On the right, Compton's battalion would initially stay behind the infantry, but then pass them and lead the infantry to Essey and Pannes.[19] Aside from his American forces, Patton also laid out the mission for the French tankers in his brigade. The French units, made up of the 14th and 17th Tank Groups, were under the command of Commandant (Major)

C. M. M. Chanoine. These two French units were the third battalion of the brigade and operated directly under Patton's command. The French tankers operated with the 4th Corps and directly for the 42d Infantry Division.[20] With the plan made and ready to go, Patton had one more fight before the battle could begin.

Prior to attack, Patton wanted a smoke screen to shield his advancing tanks, and he went through the proper channels to get one. On 8 September, four days before the scheduled attack, an impatient and anxious Patton hounded the 42nd Division's operations officer, Major Grayson M. P. Murphy, only to hear that his request had been denied—that Murphy "could not put smoke in plan as stencil was already cut."[21] It seems that Murphy was in no mood to be bothered by an overbearing tank officer, and the situation had to be appealed to higher authorities. This was an early example of how Patton's new tank units had to overcome not just enemy obstacles but Allied and American officers failing to understand how tanks operate. Major Murphy, like nearly every officer in the United States Army, was unlikely ever to have seen a tank move or to understand any tank doctrine. This was also another example of Patton showing the lack of professional maturity and the bombastic attitude that could and would land him in trouble in both world wars. In this instance Rockenbach ultimately stepped in and got the smoke screen. It was made possible, certainly, by his rank as a brigadier general, but Rockenbach's calmer and cooler demeanor and maturity confirm why he was the chief of the United States Tank Corps and Patton was just a brigade commander. As in World War II, Patton was much better suited to command an army than an army group, largely because he lacked the patience and political ability that other general officers like Omar Bradley and even Mark W. Clark possessed.

With the situation at headquarters resolved, Patton had to fight for more tanks, and there was nothing anyone could do to fix that situation. Since American-made tanks arrived only after the war, the American Expeditionary Force was to receive 225 light tanks from the French. Of those light tanks, Patton received 144, and he planned to put them all to use. Before going into battle, Patton gave another speech which gives further insight into his character and preparation before battle: "AMERICAN TANKS DO NOT SURRENDER. . . . As long as one tank is able to move it must go forward. Its presence will save the lives of hundreds of infantry and kill many Germans. Finally This is our BIG CHANCE; WHAT WE HAVE WORKED FOR . . . MAKE IT WORTH WHILE."[22]

Finally the day of the attack had arrived. On 12 September at around 5:00 a.m., 550,000 doughboys and 3.3 million artillery rounds launched their attack on the St. Mihiel salient.[23] Like all plans in war, the plans changed instantly, depending on German resistance or lack thereof and mechanical issues with Patton's tanks. When a company of tanks from the 327th Battalion arrived late, Patton, for one of the few times, blamed the French. After the battle he wrote that "the French made every mistake they could, sending trains to the wrong place or not sending them at all. The last company of the 327th Battalion detrained at 3:15 A.M. and marched right into action."[24] It was not a great start for Patton or his brigade, but the unit and its commander were resilient and overcame the friction and fog of the early part of the attack.

While the tanks were late to arrive, the operation as a whole was going well for the Americans. The attack started with more than nine hundred guns opening up on the enemy for more than four hours. However, due to the rain, mud, and fog, Patton had a tough time observing his tanks and their crews. He did not like what he was seeing. Because of the heavy downpour the tanks were moving more slowly and having a harder time with the terrain than anticipated. Also, while he did not yet understand, the tanks were using up much more gasoline because of the harsh conditions. Patton observed atop a hill and wrote: "I could see them coming along and getting stuck in the trenches. It was a most irritating sight. . . . I decided I had to see something so I took an officer and three runners and started forward. . . . I found the French stuck in a pass under shell fire I talked to the Major and went on I had not gone 200 feet when a 6" shell struck the tank he was on and killed 15 men. I went on towards Essey and got into the front line infantry who were lay down."[25]

Patton, just like his brigade, got his first taste of combat. "When the shelling first started, I had some doubts about the advisability of sticking my head over the parapet, but it is just like taking a cold bath, once you get in its all right. And I soon got out on the parapet."[26] By 9:15 a.m., Patton was growing weary of staying behind the front line and faced what historians and military officers call the "dilemma of command." As commander, Patton was debating internally whether he should stay put near his headquarters, which would allow him access to all communications with his forces and superiors, or move out and command the force personally. Despite being a lieutenant colonel and commander of a tank brigade, the excitement of the battle and the urge to prove he was courageous were too much for Patton to ignore. Following Compton's message concerning the 327th Tank Battalion, Patton decided to leave his command post and see what was going on for himself.

Moving on foot toward the action, Patton immediately saw the wrath of war, as dead soldiers lay scattered across the field. As for his tanks, he came upon a few stuck in the mud and trenches, but so far they were performing well. After he passed a few villages or hamlets, an explosive shell almost killed Patton, but he continued on. "I admit that I wanted to duck and probably did at first but soon saw the futility of dodging fate, besides I was the only officer around who had left on his shoulder straps and I had to live up to them."[27] After passing more settlements, Patton eventually met up with some French tankers under his command around St. Baussant. He also met up with Brigadier General Douglas MacArthur, commander of the 84th Infantry Brigade, and the two stood on a hill as bullets whizzed by. Patton wrote in great detail to his wife about the meeting upon a tiny hill with the famous MacArthur.

> Here I met Gen MacArthur (Douglas) commanding a brigade he was walking about too so we stood and talked but neither was much interested in what the other said as we could not get our minds off the shells. I went up a hill to have a look and could see the Bosch running beyond Essey fast then five tanks of my right Battalion came up so I told them to go through Essey. Some damned Frenchmen at the bridge told them to go back as there were too many shells in the town. The Lt in command obeyed. This made me mad so I led them through on foot but there was no danger as the Bosch shelling the next town.
>
> I asked him (MacArthur) if I could go on and attack the next town Pannes he said sure so I started. All the tanks but one ran out of gas. When we got to Pannes some two miles the infantry would not go in so I told the sgt. commanding the tank to go in. He was nearvous [sic] at being alone so I said I will sit on the roof this reassured [sic] him and we entered the town Lt. Knowles and Sgt. Graham sat on the tail of the tank.[28]

The meeting is rather remarkable. It is easy to imagine these two standing with one another and there is little doubt that their meeting did indeed occur. Many versions of this story exist, even one by MacArthur, who after World War II said that Patton flinched as one shell came over, whereupon he told Patton, "Don't worry, major, you never hear the one that gets you."[29] By the time of MacArthur's quote, Patton was dead, and MacArthur, as he showed throughout his career and as his military exploits revealed, was prone to self-promotion. It is possible MacArthur's comments on their meeting are accurate, but the quote, so long after the war, is unlikely to be true. At that stage in his life MacArthur understood how famous he and Patton had become and there was little malice in his statement toward Patton. As Patton's record in the war would bear out, while he was scared, he never showed it. There is no issue with being scared, despite what the great Douglas MacArthur stated. Every soldier and officer to ever step foot in combat is scared. How they deal with that fear is what generally makes a good soldier or officer. As a commander and officer, Patton knew that to be successful he had to heed Stonewall Jackson's dictum "Never take counsel of your fears." Most likely he did and the two men went their separate ways, both happy to get out of enemy fire. Regardless, a well-placed artillery round on that cold, rainy September day could have ended the lives of two great World War II leaders.

After talking with MacArthur, Patton moved toward the action near the villages of Essey and Pannes. When Patton's tanks reached Essey, townsfolk told the soldiers that the bridge was mined, so they turned back.[30] Soon afterward Patton met these soldiers who were afraid to cross a bridge they thought to be mined, so Patton took command of the tanks and "walked across ahead of the first tank. He then started toward Pannes with three tanks, accompanied by his reconnaissance officer and one runner."[31]

After the war, stories circulated about the bridge and how Patton so heroically crossed the mined bridge on foot. While Patton surely played up this story, his biographer Martin Blumenson believed that the bridge was probably not mined and that the story is part of the Patton legend. However, at the time of the event, Patton could not have been completely confident that the bridge was not mined. Nevertheless, Patton was leading by example and like all great leaders took the first steps to show his troops everything was fine.

When Patton and a few tanks got to Pannes, their fighting was not done for the day. According to the brigade's report after the battle, "Col. Patton, Lieut. Knowles and Sgt. Graham, climbed on top of the tank and entered the town, while the Infantry worked around the flanks. . . . Lieut. Knowles and Sgt. Graham dismounted to chase a German they saw running into a house. They entered the house and captured twenty Germans. The tank passed through the town, and, on the eastern edge Col. Patton was forced to dismount by machine gun fire, which was hitting the tank."[32]

Forced to dismount, indeed. After crossing the bridge, Patton had hitched a ride on a nearby tank as they traveled past Essey and Pannes. A few miles out of town, while still on the top of the tank, Patton noticed paint chips beginning to fly and immediately jumped off into a shell hole. Patton recounted the incident to his obviously worried wife. "I saw the paint fly off the side of the tank and heard machine guns so I jumped off and got in a shell hole it was small and the bullets nocked all of the front edge in on me."[33] Patton had to now think quickly if he wanted to escape with his life. Lying in the shell hole, Patton realized the tank he was riding on failed to notice his hurried departure and had moved forward, leaving him in a wide-open field with infantry troops far behind. Stuck in a shell hole, Patton would once again press his luck and show tremendous courage or, as some would call it, foolhardiness.

> Here I was nearvous the tank had not seen me get off and was going on. The infantry was about 200 m. back of me and did not advance. One runner on my right got hit. If I went back the infantry would think I was running if I did not they would not support the tank it might get hurt. Besides m[achine] g[un] bullets are unpleasant to hear finally I decided that I could get back obliquely. So I started as soon as the m.g's opened I would lay down and beat the bullets each time.[34]

After his "bright thought" and escape, Patton rejoined the infantry and began organizing an attack on the town of Beney. By luck, skill, or a miracle, Patton had managed to get to safety. At this point he was relieved to see that four more tanks had arrived. Putting Lieutenant Knowles into one of the tanks to supervise the next attack, Patton sent the tanks into action and asked the infantry if they would follow. The infantry happily obliged. Patton, now without a tank or motorized vehicle, decided to walk along the lines of battle to the left flank at the village of Nonsard. On the way Patton found twenty-five tanks and discovered his brigade had lost four men and two officers. Making the next operation harder, all the tanks with Patton were out of gas. Here again Patton showed great leadership and led by example. Without any aides, runners, or vehicles, Patton decided he was the only one who could get back to the rear area and get more gas to his tanks: "All my runners were gone so I started back seven miles to tell them to get some gas. That was the only bad part of the fight I had no sleep for two nights and nothing to eat since the night before except some crackers I got off a dead Bosch. I would have given a lot for a little brandy but even my water was gone."[35]

Patton did manage to find a motorcycle along the way and was able to get gas brought forward for his tanks and even make a report to the Corps headquarters.

Around 3:00 p.m., exhausted but content with the progression of the battle, Patton sat down for his first meal, only to find that a German POW had replaced his hamper sack with rocks. Following the taking of Beney, both the 326th and 327th Tank Battalions settled in for the night. The first day of the attack had been immensely successful, and the St. Mihiel salient was no more.

The next day Patton and his tanks moved forward and found little to no German resistance. On 14 September, Patton's forces found some German resistance near the town of Jonville on the vaunted Hindenburg Line. Wasting no time, as in World War II when he rushed forces to be the first to the Rhine, Patton ordered five tanks to attack and take Jonville. This attack was small, but the operation earned the nickname Task Force McClure. The small unit of five tanks led by Second Lieutenant Edwin A. McClure showed Patton, for the first time, that in the future tanks could operate independent of infantry. McClure was able to attack a German infantry regiment, seize their light machine guns, capture four 77-millimeter guns, and drive the Germans back nearly six kilometers.[36] Task Force McClure was able to do this by its willingness to attack the Germans directly, and it did so without infantry support. This was a rare event in World War I, mainly because the tanks did not break down or run out of gas. When well supported and maintained, tanks could wage and win battles without infantry support. Task Force McClure was the exception to the rule in World War I, but it foreshadowed what was to come in World War II.

While the St. Mihiel battle was over, Patton's raid on Jonville and the Hindenburg Line was the first time American tankers had defeated German ground forces independently. Some critics would argue that this move was pointless and was ordered only to feed Patton's ego, but Patton understood the amazing effects that victory against the enemy brought his troops. While only seizing a small town, the victory certainly raised morale and also told the French, British, and Germans that the American Expeditionary Force was a well-trained army that could fight anyone, anywhere.

With the battle over, Patton began the arduous process of compiling what could be learned. For the Americans the battle of St. Mihiel was a tremendous success: 16,000 Germans and 450 guns were captured and more than 7,000 Germans were killed, wounded, or missing. On the American side, only a few hundred deaths were reported. Most important, the victory "probably did more than any single operation of the war to encourage the tired allies."[37] As for Patton's 177 tanks engaged in the battle along with 33 French tanks, Patton remarked "total losses for the 3 days 4 men killed 4 men & 4 officers wounded. Two Tanks smashed."[38] With only four killed in action and eight wounded, Patton's tank forces had done extremely well without much loss of life and equipment.

Following the battle, and later the war, the brigade wrote a lengthy and detailed history of the 304th Tank Brigade's performance at St. Mihiel that served as an after-action report of Patton's unit. The history, likely written by Patton along with Brett, recorded: "On Sept. 12, the attack came off as planned, so far as the Tanks were concerned. Due to the slight resistance offered by the Germans, there was no real test of the ability of the tanks as fighting machines. However, the 344th Bn. reached its final objective—Nonsard—with the Infantry, and Major Brett, commanding the Battalion, shot a German machine gun crew out of the church steeple of that town."[39]

The losses were relatively light, especially for a first-time unit, but there were some issues with the tank, and improvements in training and manufacturing needed to be made. In general, the light tanks all had major problems crossing the enemy trenches, reflecting one of the biggest issues with tank warfare in World War I. While Patton and other tank commanders understood the limitations of the tanks, most of the American and Allied commanders did not. Patton realized this, and since joining the Tank Corps he had worked to try to bridge the gap of knowledge with other officers, but the task was rendered impossible by the sheer size and ever growing strength of the American Expeditionary Force. To make matters worse, most senior officers in the Allies' armies had little regard for light tanks, and those officers who did hope to use tanks had very little knowledge of how to employ them and how they operated.

The width of the German trenches proved to be too much for many light tanks at St. Mihiel, especially the French tanks in Patton's brigade. "The French tanks had great difficulty in crossing the trenches, and never succeeded in passing the Infantry, though they made splendid efforts." They were not alone in their difficulties. "Tanks designed to cross six-foot trenches were made to cross trenches from ten to fourteen feet wide, and not only one, but trench after trench."[40] It was rather remarkable that most of the Americans' Renault tanks were able to successfully cross the trenches. This proved to Patton that the training center he had established was working and his soldiers were performing admirably.

One of the biggest factors in tank warfare in World War I was the ability of the infantry and the Tank Corps to work together. At St. Mihiel the two branches worked well with each other at times, but often the infantry were unwilling to move forward with the tanks. This made life difficult and dangerous for Patton's tankers. However, there were examples of good coordination between the two branches. Tanks from the 327th Battalion had trouble crossing the wider German trenches at the Tranchée d'Houblons, east of St. Baussant, but five tanks were able to cross and enter the village of Essey with infantry support, and the same force took nearby Pannes an hour later.[41] At St. Mihiel, when the United States Tank Corps worked very well with the infantry, much of the credit was due not to great planning or teamwork but to a lack of German resistance.

Many individuals of Patton's brigade showed great leadership and bravery. One of the most amazing feats of bravery in the war happened in Alpha Company of the 326th Battalion. Captain Semmes, the company commander, was riding in a tank when it fell into the Rupt de Mad, northeast of Richecourt. According to the brigade's report: "The tank was completely submerged. Captain Semmes escaped by the turret door and started to swim ashore when he noted that his driver was still in the tank. Despite the fact that some German were firing at him from the trenches nearby, Capt. Semmes returned to his tank, dove into it, and rescued the driver by dragging him out by the ears. The two then swam ashore and killed one of the Germans."[42] For his act of heroism, Captain Semmes would be awarded the Distinguished Service Cross.

Patton's chief lieutenant, and most reliable battalion commander once in combat, Major Sereno Brett, who had long shown his value as a trainer, now showed his professionalism and expertise in combat. Tanks and crews under Brett's command had difficulty in moving toward their objective in the right direction due to the rain, mud, and poor visibility, forcing Brett to lead his command on foot. This was not unique to Brett; many officers did the same thing. Often they had no choice, since the Renault tanks had poor sight lines, and in poor weather tanks and their crews would wander off course. Brett, however, continued to lead on foot for "several kilometers in the face of machine gun and rifle fire; setting a fine example of coolness and courage to all his command."[43] Following

Major Brett's lead, First Lieutenant Julian K. Morrison led his platoon in attack against German machine-gun nests on foot and with pistol in hand, was wounded twice, but was able to accomplish the mission.

Major Chanoine, the commander of the French tank groups, was nearly killed by a 150-millimeter shell just east of Maizerais when the shell scored a direct hit against a nearby tank. Chanoine was blown away from the tank and was found unconscious but alive.[44] He quickly recovered and soon returned to duty.

Aside from personnel losses, Patton's brigade was running low on working tanks. After the battle, the brigade counted its material losses and discovered "Besides the three tanks destroyed, twenty-two were ditched so badly that they were out of action all day, and fourteen had bad mechanical trouble. This was out of one hundred and seventy-seven tanks entering the action with the 304th Brigade."[45] It was during the battle that the 301st Repair and Salvage Company earned their pay, working nearly nonstop to help get damaged tanks back into action.

While 12 September 1918 had seen the most action for the brigade, there was still a need for tanks in the American sector. Due to loss of tanks and a lack of German resistance, Patton and the 304th Tank Brigade saw little action on 13 September. Making matters worse for the United States Tank Corps, the condition of the roads and the traffic made it impossible for the corps's resupply of gasoline to arrive in time. On 14 September, twenty-two French tanks and one American Renault tank of the 345th Battalion were called into action and seized St. Benoît.[46] On the same day, near St. Maurice, lucky American tankers found German blankets and cigars. In addition to the captured German goods, Major Brett "accidently" captured two Austrian soldiers who managed to walk right into Brett as he led his tanks on foot. Besides the blankets, cigars, and Austrians, American soldiers found a human finger that was still warm.[47] By the end of 14 September, Patton ordered his tanks to withdraw to the Bois de Thiaucourt, roughly twelve kilometers from the front. Here the brigade rested and saw no major combat for the rest of the St. Mihiel operation.[48]

While the fighting in St. Mihiel was rather light, as the Germans had vacated many of the defensive positions, the battle was highly successful for the American Expeditionary Force, the 304th Tank Brigade, and Patton. The performance of the tanks, while far from perfect, proved to doubters that tanks were an important and powerful weapon, not just a laboring machine. As for Patton's view, he believed he and his forces had done well but could do better. "In spite of very serious obstacles of terrain the tanks were in a position to aid the Infantry and would have done so had such resistance been necessary. As it was, the tanks entered the town of Nonsard, Pannes, and Beney ahead of the Infantry and captured the town of Jonville unaided by any Infantry whatever."[49]

Personally, Patton believed he showed courage under fire and tremendous leadership qualities. Patton wrote glowingly to his wife after the battle, "I at least proved to my own satisfaction that I have nerve. I was the only man on the front line except gen. McArthur who never ducked a shell. I wanted to but it is foolish as it does no good if they are going to hit you they will." Unfortunately, General Rockenbach believed Patton's conduct during the battle was less than exemplary. As Patton put it, "Gen R. gave me hell for going up but it had to be done at least I will not sit in a dug out and have my men out in the fighting."[50]

As a tank brigade commander, Patton's duty was at headquarters, not running around in a field chasing tanks. In Rockenbach's reprimand of Patton's conduct he made three points: "1) the five light tanks of a platoon had to work together, had to be kept intact under the platoon commander, and not be allowed to be split up; 2) when a tank brigade was allotted to a corps, the commander was to remain at the corps headquarters or be in close telephonic communications with it; 3) 'I wish you would especially impress on your men that they are fighting [with] tanks, they are not Infantry, and any man who abandons his Tank will in the future be tried.'"[51]

While it is understandable for a man of Patton's personality and makeup to be with his soldiers, not safe in a command post, Rockenbach's points are essentially correct. An officer in Patton's position is a link in the command, and without him near a telephone or runners, this link is broken and can dramatically impact an operation. Also, tankers are not trained infantrymen and should stay with their broken-down tanks, not join with fellow ground soldiers as infantry. Regardless of the reprimand, Patton's personal leadership during the battle endeared him to his soldiers, and in World War II, while Omar Bradley was considered the "G.I. General," it was Patton who joined the men at the front and made his presence felt. Where Rockenbach considered Patton's wandering off to the front line a weakness, Viner considered it a strength, "George Patton was always on the front lines, never in the rear with the Red Cross. That was one of the secrets to his greatness."[52]

As word of the Americans' success made it around the world, Patton and his brigade received numerous letters and memos of congratulations from senior officers. Perhaps the most important to Patton professionally were the kind words from his mentor and the American Expeditionary Force commander, General John J. Pershing: "Please accept my sincere congratulations on the successful and important part taken by the officers and men of the Tank Corps in the first offensive of the First American Army on September 12th and 13th. The courageous dash and vigor of our troops has thrilled our countrymen and evoked the enthusiasm of our allies. Please convey to your command my heartfelt appreciation of their splendid work. I am proud of you all."[53]

Patton, also received a short message from his boss, Brigadier General Samuel Rockenbach. Up to this point the two had clashed, but together they had formed the backbone of the Tank Corps and laid the foundation for its success. Following the battle at St. Mihiel, Rockenbach wrote a brief letter to Patton congratulating the 304th Tank Brigade on its success:

In addition to this, express to them my appreciation of the hard, laborious and excellent work which was done by your Brigade prior to the engagement and then to the dash and vim of their attack in which you were so ably assisted by the IV Group Schneider, French. Preceding our Infantry you not only saved them many losses, but by planting your red, yellow, and blue flag well in advance and on the Hindenburg line you had a very great, farreaching and disastrous effect on the enemy.

Your brigade has, in their baptism of fire, established a record that the corps will, by its best endeavors, attempt to perpetuate.[54]

Never one to rest on his laurels, Patton realized much of the victory was due not to his leadership, or the might of the tank, but to a lack of German resistance. There was an empty feeling to St. Mihiel, and Patton knew it. Luckily for him and his tank brigade, he would not have to wait long to prove his mettle. This time the German resistance would be stiff and the fighting hard.

With the St. Mihiel salient shattered, the American Expeditionary Force and Patton's brigade immediately readied themselves for the next move, the Meuse-Argonne offensive. Ten American divisions would attack in the first wave, while eight others waited in reserve.[55] Collectively, the AEF faced eighteen German divisions, roughly 125,000 troops. Following an artillery bombardment, the AEF forces were to attack from south to north against a small area twenty miles wide and thirteen miles long.[56] Throughout this area were countless German defensive fortifications, dugouts, and other obstacles. For his tanks, Patton devised a plan for a concentrated thrust through the enemy defenses. The 304th Tank Brigade was ordered to support the 28th and 35th Divisions of the United States 1st Corps as they attacked from the west. With Brett's 344th Tank Battalion leading, followed by Compton's 345th Tank Battalion, the two units would break out of the line and advance as far as they could. Immediately after the breakout, Patton wanted French ground forces to follow the tanks toward their objectives. With 140 tanks at his disposal, Patton's plan was not revolutionary, but his theories on tanks were maturing and showed a more aggressive approach than at St. Mihiel.

Fox Conner was a major influence on Patton's career before
World War I and after. Conner was one of the United States
Army's most able officers prior to World War II. (National
Archives, 111-SC-14033)

Colonel LeRoy Eltinge helped steer Patton toward tanks
during the war and helped establish the United States
Tank Corps. (National Archives, 111-SC-14031)

Colonel Samuel D. Rockenbach, soon to be promoted to brigadier general, was the chief of the United States Tank Corps during and after World War I. He constantly clashed with his subordinate George S. Patton Jr. (National Archives, 111-SC-14047)

(*Above*) The Renault tank was the light tank for the United States Army in World War I and was personally selected for service by George S. Patton Jr. (National Archives, 111-SC-15524) (*Below*) A lone soldier walks through the Tank Corps training facility at Camp Colt, Gettysburg, PA. (National Archives, 111-SC-15526)

(*Above*) An official hand-drawn sketch of Chaumont by Captain J. Andre Smith. (National Archives, 111-SC-15544) (*Below)* Patton's tanks were constantly slowed by the poor condition of the roads and the intense traffic. World War I tanks were better supported by rail. (National Archives, 111-SC-22328)

(*Above*) Americans drive their Renault tanks to the front. (National Archives, 111-SC-22334) (*Below*) American tanks south of the 28th Infantry Division area move slowly through the Argonne Forest. (National Archives, 111-SC-22330)

(*Above*) French decorations (*top, left to right*): Croix de Guerre, Médaille Militaire, Légion d'Honneur; British decorations (*bottom, left to right*): Military Cross, Victoria Cross, Distinguished Conduct Medal, Military Medal. (National Archives, 111-SC-22420) (*Below*) A tank from Patton's brigade stuck in a trench. (National Archives, 111-SC-22493)

German dummy tanks designed after British Mark tanks. (National Archives, 111-SC-22674)

Head shot of George S. Patton Jr. circa 1916. (Library of Congress, Patton Papers, Box 60, Folder 14)

(*Above*) Patton sits for a photo with Brett's 344th Tank Battalion. (Library of Congress, Patton Papers, Box 61, Folder 8) (*Below*) Group shot of the United States Tank Corps, Fort Meade, MD, circa 1919. Patton sits beside Dwight D. Eisenhower. (Library of Congress, Patton Papers, Box 60, Folder 13)

(*Above*) An American tank crew driving a Renault tank. (Library of Congress, Patton Papers, Box 61, Folder 8) (*Below*) Two Renault tanks for the United States Tank Corps. (Library of Congress, Patton Papers, Box 61, Folder 8)

(*Above*) American soldiers help clean a Renault tank. (Library of Congress, Patton Papers, Box 61, Folder 8) (*Below*) American soldiers clean and a repair a Renault tank. (Library of Congress, Patton Papers, Box 61, Folder 8)

(*Above*) American tanks drive toward the front lines during the Meuse-Argonne campaign. (Library of Congress, Patton Papers, Box 61, Folder 8) (*Below*) American tank crews conceal their tanks with netting. (Library of Congress, Patton Papers, Box 61, Folder 8)

(*Above*) American tanks parked outside the town of Varennes. (Library of Congress, Patton Papers, Box 61, Folder 8) (*Below*) A destroyed Renault tank. (Library of Congress, Patton Papers, Box 61, Folder 8)

(*Above*) An American tank crew in action. Soldiers dodge shells in Exermont. (Library of Congress, Patton Papers, Box 61, Folder 8) (*Below*) A Whippet, or Medium Mark A, another tank in action during World War I. (Library of Congress, Patton Papers, Box 61, Folder 8)

(*Above*) Part of a tank company starting a maneuver. (Library of Congress, Patton Papers, Box 61, Folder 8) (*Below*) A Renault tank seen head on. (Library of Congress, Patton Papers, Box 61, Folder 8)

(*Above*) United States Army tank officers with crew. Standing in the center, facing away, is Patton. (Library of Congress, Patton Papers, Box 61, Folder 8) (*Below*) A Renault tank drives out of a trench. (Library of Congress, Patton Papers, Box 61, Folder 8)

(*Above*) Relative size of a light tank and a soldier. (National Archives at College Park, MD, SC 17546) (*Below*) An American Renault tank and assorted traffic slowly cross a hastily repaired bridge. (Library of Congress, Patton Papers, Box 61, Folder 8)

(*Above*) American soldiers lying prone, with a British Mark tank in the distance. (Library of Congress, Patton Papers, Box 61, Folder 8) (*Below*) A British heavy tank. Patton preferred the speed and reliability of the lighter Renault tanks. (Library of Congress, Patton Papers, Box 61, Folder 8)

(*Above*) An American tanker drives his muddy Renault forward. (Library of Congress, Patton Papers, Box 61, Folder 8) (*Below*) An American heavy tank rolls on. (Library of Congress, Patton Papers, Box 61, Folder 8)

(*Above*) A German blueprint of a Whippet tank discovered by American soldiers. (Library of Congress, Patton Papers, Box 61, Folder 8) (*Below*) American "training tanks." (Library of Congress, Patton Papers, Box 61, Folder 8)

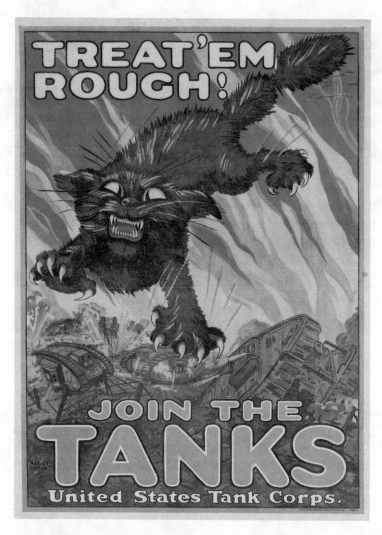

United States Tank Corps recruiting poster. (Library of Congress, Patton Papers, Box 61, Folder 9)

WAR DEPARTMENT TELEGRAM.

OFFICIAL BUSINESS.

WASHINGTON. October 12,1918

AGSD 201 (Patton, George S,Jr.)

George S Patton,
San Gabriel, Cal.

Deeply regret to inform you that it is officially

reported that Major George S. Patton,Jr. Cavalry.

was   wounded in action Degree undetermined,September Twenty-sixth

Department has no further information.

354-269-60-2
MAH

Harris
Acting The Adjutant General

Telegram informing Patton's father of his son's wounding. (National Archives, Digital Identifier no. 57302258)

(*Above*) Patton (*left*) stands with other United States Tank Corps officers. (Virginia Military Institute Archives, Samuel Rockenbach Papers, Box 6, Photographs, Folder 6A) (*Below*) Patton stands in front of a Renault tank with another United States Tank Corps officer, probably Salerno Brett. (Virginia Military Institute Archives, Samuel Rockenbach Papers, Box 6, Photographs, Folder 6A)

(*Above*) Colonel Patton proudly stands in front of a Renault tank. (Virginia Military Institute Archives, Samuel Rockenbach Papers, Box 6, Photographs, Folder 6A) (*Below*) An American tanker and his tank appear to have capsized. (Virginia Military Institute Archives, Samuel Rockenbach Papers, Box 6, Photographs, Folder 18)

5

The True Test

The Meuse-Argonne Offensive
(15 September–10 October 1918)

> It is funny how one's mind works. I would never have gone
> forward when I got hit had I not thought of you and my
> ancestors. I felt that I could not be false to my "cast" and your
> opinion.
> —Patton to Beatrice Patton, 24 October 1918

The Meuse-Argonne offensive was a massive undertaking, and would be
the largest operation by the United States Army in World War I. Much
larger in size and scope than St. Mihiel, it had a small but important role
for the 304th Tank Brigade. After receiving some guidance from higher
headquarters on 15 September, Patton and his staff first had to survey the
ground and make sure it was suitable for tanks. At this point in the war, it
had become clear to Patton and Rockenbach that one of the main duties
of tank commanders was to survey the terrain with an eye to tank activ-
ity. This was mainly due, once again, to the infantry's unfamiliarity with
tanks. In September 1918, very few infantry officers understood what
tanks could and could not do. Generally they paid little attention to the
terrain and the width of the sector. Often tank commanders like Patton
would have to narrow down the width of their sector as they did not have
enough tanks. Another major issue was the point of debarkation. World
War I tanks could not travel far without wasting gasoline and breaking
down. Using the road network was nearly impossible, given the mud and
traffic. For tanks to succeed in the war, they had to detrain as close as
possible to the front lines. This issue would bedevil Patton and his commanders throughout the war.

As for the battle plan, the 304th Tank Brigade was attached to the
First United States Army. Patton did not like what he initially saw. He
scouted the 1st Corps sector and found the terrain "more or less unfavor-

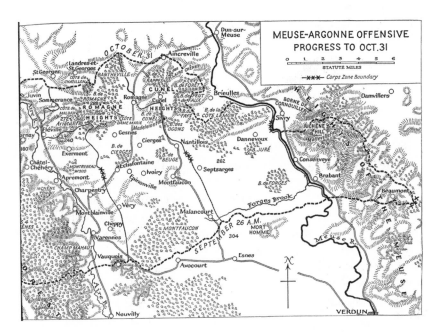

Source: Meuse-Argonne Offensive: (John J. Pershing, *My Experiences in the World War,* vol. 2 [New York: Stokes, 1931], 352).

able to tanks until the line Montblainville-Ivory had been passed," while the sector between the Forêt d'Argonne and the Bois de Cheppy, a front of about three kilometers, was the least difficult.[1] It was in this area that the 35th Infantry Division was to attack east of the Aire River, while the 28th Infantry Division was to attack west of the river. In the 28th Infantry Division's sector, Patton felt that there was minimal room for tanks and the ground could support only one tank company.

Patton outlined the attack as he did for the St. Mihiel offensive. The 344th Tank Battalion was ordered to lead the attack as far as the First Army could go. Alpha Company and Charlie Company of the 344th Tank Battalion were sent east of the Aire River and attached to the 35th Infantry Division. Bravo Company was tasked with fighting on the unfavorable ground in the 28th Infantry Division's sector west of the Aire River.[2]

As for the 345th Tank Battalion, Patton decided, as he did with the 344th, to split the battalion between two fronts. Bravo and Charlie Companies were ordered to the east, while Alpha Company was moved west of the Aire River. The companies of the 345th Battalion were to follow their sister battalion at a distance of roughly 1,500 meters, and their goal was again the First United States Army's objective. Once the First Army reached their destination, the 345th Battalion would "make a passage of lines with the 344th Battalion," where they would "hop" over the 344th Battalion and take the lead.

The plan was much more complex and aggressive than the attack on the St. Mihiel salient. Even in contemporary warfare, having units pass other units is a rather complex and risky operation. However, the 304th Tank Brigade had shown it was ready for such an undertaking, and Patton was confident the action would go roughly as he intended. To alleviate the gasoline issues that plagued his tank brigade at St. Mihiel, Patton made a bold, and rather shocking, plan to give his tanks extra fuel. Patton ordered that "each tank moving into action was required to carry two 20-liter cans tied to its tail. This created some danger from fire, but the risk was thought preferable to the lack of gas."[3] Certainly a fire hazard, the new idea worked well during the operation, and there were no reported casualties due to dragging large quantities of gasoline.

Prior to the attack, Patton wrote to his wife and once again compared war and combat to sport, saying his fear of war was akin to that of playing polo. "I am always nearvous about this time as at Polo or at Foot ball before the game starts but so far I have been all right after that."[4] By 26 September, as the Meuse-Argonne attack was hours away, Patton had to deal with two major issues. First, Captain Compton's battalion failed to show up on schedule, and for a brief time Patton and his staff lost communication with the battalion and had no idea where they were. Patton vented to his wife, writing, "Life is just one D— thing after another one whole Battalion has failed to show up and I can't find it." Patton opined that maybe he was not suited for command. "Some times I think I am not such a great commander after all. Just a fighting animal. Still I will improve in time at least if one learns by mistakes I ought to be wise I have made all there are."[5] Compton's battalion did arrive, just in time for the operation.

In the meantime, Patton was dealt another blow that led him to further question his capacity for command. This time, however, it was not due to any of Patton's failings or his subordinates', but rather simply small mistakes in war that can often snowball and lead to great mishaps. After dealing with gasoline shortages during St. Mihiel, the United States Tank Corps pushed for and received more gasoline than originally anticipated. On 26 September, as Patton was looking for his lost battalion, his brigade received 10,000 gallons of gas. Instead of being overjoyed with the support, Patton was perplexed when it was discovered that the gas cars had arrived but did not have their dippers.[6] For a few hours Patton's tank brigade had more gas than they could want, but they had no means to fill their tanks! Just hours away from the start of the largest operation the Americans had undertaken in their history, Patton was left to deal with issues that further complicated his plans.

The Meuse-Argonne offensive finally got under way during the early morning of 26 September in a heavy fog as the artillery bombardment began. Almost immediately as the tankers and infantry moved out, they faced devastating German machine-gun and artillery fire. The weather was not ideal for infantry and even less so for the tanks. With the fog so heavy, the tanks quickly lost contact with each other, and Patton, who for the moment was staying behind after his tongue-lashing by Rockenbach, had trouble viewing his command. In the midst of the largest attack by the United States in World War I, Patton had time to write a quick diary entry, recording that his force "was fired on heavily and 35 Div came back on the run. Moved back about 200 m. Heavy m.g. & Art. Fire lots of Dough Boys hit. English & I got tanks forward. 20 men hit."[7] Despite the fog and heavy German fire, Patton was happy with the performance of his tanks. They were making slow but steady progress for nearly four hours until, around 10 a.m., the German defense slowed the tanks along Patton's narrow front.

Just after the start of the attack, Patton technically disregarded Rockenbach's order and reprimand and left his command post to see how his tanks were performing. As best he could make out in the fog, it seemed his brigade needed a shove, so he left for the front with Captain English, commander of Company C, 344th Battalion. Patton, as he and his company and battalion commanders regularly did, hopped on top of a Renault tank parapet and assisted some of his tanks in crossing wide trenches. Both Patton and English sat on the tank as gunfire and artillery fire exploded all around. Patton then ordered English and his company to proceed in the direction of Cheppy. The tanks moved forward, but when the infantry attempted to follow, they were taken in the flank by the Germans as they crossed a small ridge in the battlefield.[8]

Hopping off the tank, Patton followed tank tracks on the Clermont-Neuvilly-Boureuilles-Varennes road and after a few kilometers met up with some more of his tanks. After they talked, the tankers they moved on and Patton resumed his walk to the front. Almost immediately German artillery shells hit, followed by machine-gun fire, and everyone hit the dirt. Patton ordered all ground troops toward a railroad cut.

During this difficult time, west of Patton's position, Company B of the 344th Battalion was dealing with a tough situation as well. Company B had made decent progress and entered the town of Varennes at 9:30 a.m., but once again the nfantry failed to support the tanks. The reason was not a lack of courage or training but German machine-gun fire that opened up from the Forêt d'Argonne and stopped the infantry from advancing. Bravo Company was left on its own until after 1:30 p.m., when the infantry finally made it into Varennes. This was a dangerous few hours for Captain Weed and his company. Sometime during the hours without infantry support, Weed himself was briefly taken prisoner by the Germans as he was reconnoitering ahead of his tanks. Luckily for Weed and his company, one of Weed's tanks showed up as if on cue and scared the Germans away, giving Captain Weed just enough time to reverse direction and escape permanent capture.[9]

While Captain Weed and his B Company fought for their survival, Patton was lying prone with about two hundred infantrymen. Not one to lie down longer than he needed to, Patton attempted to get the men to advance, but he found that quite difficult, as he wrote to Beatrice. "There were no officers there but me. So I decided to do business. Some of my reserve tanks were stuck by some trenches. So I went back and made some Americans hiding in the trenches dig a passage."[10] The work was slow going, and Patton began to grow frustrated. "It being impossible to get them to advance, Col. Patton called for volunteers to attack the machine guns. Seven out of about 200 men present advanced with him, but were all hit—the last about forty meters from the guns. A French tank then moved forward, but struck a mine and was destroyed. Finally a platoon of American tanks got by the ditch."[11]

Once in the safety of the cut, Patton waited for the firing to end, as more and more infantry troops began running from the front, seeking protection in the cut with Patton and his group of soldiers. With the attack dying down, Patton noticed tanks stopped before a large trench. Seizing the letup in the German bombardment, Patton organized the near hundred of infantrymen and marched them to the trench. As they approached the trench, Patton ordered everyone to once again hit the dirt, as machine-gun bullets flew over their heads. After the fire died down again, Patton immediately ordered the men to help get the tanks across the trench, and the men began to tear down the trench walls. Unfortunately, the Germans began another barrage and laid down heavy machine-gun fire. Unmoved by the firing, Patton ordered his troops to hold their ground and continue digging. While some continued to dig, others fled back to the railroad cut. Angry at this lack of courage, Patton continued to dig and even hit a few soldiers over the head with a shovel to keep them working. Patton wrote to his wife days later, "I think I killed one man here he would not work so I hit him over the head with a shovel."[12]

Patton demonstrated many skills acquired in World War I and only built and improved those skills during the interwar period. However, there was always a rougher, brutal side to him. In World War II, Patton twice slapped soldiers during Operation HUSKY, the invasion of Sicily led by Patton and his Seventh United States Army. The slappings created a worldwide uproar and nearly cost Patton his career and, perhaps more important, his reputation. Even by the standards of the 1940s, what Patton did was very much against social and military norms. A small statistical breakdown of letters to Patton following the slapping incidents shows the American populace divided over his conduct.[13] Those who were angry with Patton argued that it was conduct unbecoming an officer and that hitting soldiers who were injured, mentally or physically, was not acceptable for American military officers and certainly not for general officers. Those who supported Patton did not support the slappings outright but balanced the hitting of the soldiers with conduct characteristic of waging and fighting a total war. They did not excuse his behavior so much as contend that while he had made a mistake, Patton had proved himself invaluable to winning the war, and the slappings should not end his career.

As for the incident at the trench in World War I, the era in which he was serving and the war in which he was fighting were different from the slapping incidents of World War II in the 1940s. There is no doubt that Patton was incorrect to hit the soldier on the head with a shovel. However, unlike in World War II, where the slappings were done away from the battlefield and certainly not in combat, Patton hit a soldier in the middle of an intense firefight in one of the largest military operations of the war. The reason Patton's hitting incident in World War I received no attention from the army or the media was twofold. First, Patton was too junior an officer and just a cog in the American Expeditionary Force. While he had garnered some regional renown and a small national following after his vehicular attack in Mexico, Patton was largely unknown to the United States. In World War II, Patton was the Seventh Army commander, one of the highest-ranking army officers and in the most publicized position up to that point in the war. Second, with the mass media still early in their development in World War I, the news just did not get out, and even if it had, it likely would have produced few headlines. By 1918 the brutality of the war was well known to combatants and non-combatants. Both sides, the Allies and the Central Powers, had shown the ability to crush their own soldiers through severe discipline and conduct that would be viewed as illegal in World War II and in the current day.

There is no evidence that Patton ever reflected on hitting the soldier in World War I, or thought about it following the two slapping incidents. Apparently Patton did not view it as a major issue. It goes back to one of his core beliefs that made him such a great field commander: that war was serious business and there was no place for gentleness. For Patton the ends—getting the tank across the trench in World War I—were more important than the means, which included hitting the soldier. This was a subject that Patton would pay little attention to until World War II and that scholars and veterans alike have seldom mentioned in any studies.

After he hit the soldier with the shovel, Patton and his mishmash unit were able to get tanks across the trench. However, while the tanks were now moving, Patton was stuck with a couple hundred infantrymen who were looking to him for leadership and direction. Patton, as he had done throughout the war, decided to lead from the front and attack. With the fire increasing and more troops falling on either side of him, Patton pushed forward, yelling, "To Hell with them, they can't hit me!"[14] Patton wrote of what happened next in a letter back home:

> At last we got Five tanks across and I started them forward and yelled and cusses and waved my stick and said come on about 150 dough boys started but when we got the crest of the hill the fire got fierce right along the ground. We all lay down I saw that we must go forward or back and I could not go back so I yelled who comes with me. A lot of dough boys yelled but only six of us started. My striker, me and 4 doughs. I hoped the rest would follow but they would not soon there was only three but we could see the machine guns right ahead so we yelled to keep up our courage and went on. Then the third man went down and I felt a blow in the leg but at first I could walk so went about 40 feet when my leg gave way. My striker the only man left yelled, "oh god the colonels hit and there aint no one left."[15]

Patton's perspective aside, his diary entries and letters home match very well with what soldiers witnessed. When the tanks were freed of the trenches and rolled past the initial German line, Patton had readied himself and his motley group of soldiers to advance. Waving his big walking stick over his head, he tried to rally the troops and shouted, "Let's go get them, who's with me."[16] Caught in the moment, more than one hundred troops jumped to their feet and ran down the hill with Patton. After they advanced only fifty yards or so, German machine-gun fire increased, causing Patton and his soldiers to hit the dirt. With machine-gun fire growing stronger by the minute, Patton had his vision. "I felt a great desire to run, I was trembling with fear when suddenly I thought of my progenitors and seemed to see them in a cloud over the German lines looking at me. I became calm at once and saying aloud, 'It is time for another Patton to die' called for volunteers and went forward to what I honestly believed to be certain death. Six men went with me; five were killed."[17]

Patton picked himself up, waved his walking stick, and shouted to the six men following him, "Let's go, let's go!"[18] As the other men quickly fell, Patton's orderly, Private First Class Joseph T. Angelo, wondered what Patton wanted to prove: armed only with a walking stick, what could he do?[19] Forced to take cover with Angelo in a shell hole, Patton once again tried to advance. No more than a few seconds later, Patton felt the shock of a bullet entering his leg. Struggling to move, Patton managed to crawl back into the shell hole with Angelo. The time was 11:30 a.m., the place near the village of Cheppy. Angelo managed to bandage Patton's wound, and the two awaited help. While tanks and soldiers of Patton's command came by, the German machine-gun fire was too great for them to help. The best they could do was watch and hope their beloved colonel would make it out.

After a few hours the fire abated, and Patton, still conscious, was placed on a stretcher and taken to the medic tent. Although injured and suffering from massive blood loss, Patton ordered the medics to take him to 35th Division headquarters so he could give his report of the front.[20] After reporting to headquarters, Patton was sent to Hospital Number 11 and immediately operated on.

The next morning Patton awoke dazed but otherwise feeling rather good. Wounded à la Forrest Gump, Patton wrote home to his wife that he was "missing half my bottom but otherwise all right,"[21] and he described the actual wound: "The bullet went into the front of my left leg and came out just at the crack of my bottom about two inches to the left of my rectum. It was fired at about 50 m so made a hole about the size of a dollar where it came out. . . . It hurt very little and I have slepped fine I will be out in ten days."[22]

While Patton awoke in the hospital and was generally positive, his brigade had a lot of work left and a lot of fighting ahead. Unlike at St.

Mihiel, the Germans were going to stand and fight, and the 304th Tank Brigade would have to do it without Patton for the first time in its existence. With their colonel wounded and out of action, Major Brett took command of the 304th Tank Brigade, and during the rest of the battle the brigade performed rather brilliantly. As Martin Blumenson attests, Patton "had passed the final test of leadership, leaving behind him in other men the conviction and will to carry on."[23]

At the time of Patton's wounding the Meuse-Argonne offensive was facing serious difficulty. To the west, in the 28th Infantry Division's sector, just as Patton was getting pinned down, Company B of the 344th Tank Battalion entered the town of Varennes at 9:30 a.m. However, as at St. Mihiel, the tanks advanced but the infantry were slow to keep up. The 28th Infantry Division and Company B of the 344th Tank Battalion faced some of the most severe resistance in the initial phase of the battle. It was during this day that United States forces encountered, many for the first time, German-built concrete "pillboxes."[24] The pillboxes proved a tough nut to crack, but eventually American forces discovered that high-explosive 37-millimeter shells were quite successful in destroying them.

On 27 September, as Patton recovered in the hospital, his brigade confronted tough challenges. Only eleven tanks were able to support the 28th Infantry Division's advance along the eastern edge of the Argonne Forest. The following day, 28 September, fifteen tanks supported the division's advance. The tanks assigned to the 35th Infantry Division had better luck and were able to throw forty tanks, including six French tanks, into the attack. Also, five tanks acted as a liaison between the 91st and the 35th Infantry Division. Brett kept twenty-seven tanks in reserve.[25] Despite the tanks performing as expected, the United States advance was slow going, and casualties were beginning to grow.

For the 304th Tank Brigade, the fighting on 28–29 September brought severe losses in men and tanks. The 304th Brigade history, written after the battle, recorded: "Fifty of the tanks which entered the fight in the morning were put out of action during the fighting of the day. All five tanks, operating with the 91st Division were knocked out during the first hour of the fight."[26] To make matters worse, First Lieutenant E. A. Higgins, commanding the group, was blinded and knocked out of the war.

Given the high rates of casualties and equipment losses, Rockenbach, in consultation with Brett, made the tough call to send in tanks in provisional groups rather than complete companies. The loss of junior officers as well as tanks left the United States Tank Corps little choice but to deploy tanks in disjointed units. As for the French tanks assigned to Patton's 304th Tank Brigade, they had suffered more losses than their sister American units, and Rockenbach relieved the 14th and 17th Groups and ordered them to return to training areas immediately.[27]

By 29 September the 304th Tank Brigade was able to provide fifty-five tanks for the day's attack. Fifteen American light tanks were sent to the 28th Infantry Division, forty to the 35th Infantry Division. The fifteen tanks attached to the 28th Infantry Division saw the brunt of the fighting on 29 September as they faced severe German machine-gun fire along the eastern edge of the Argonne Forest.[28] As for the forty tanks attached to the 35th Infantry Division, Captain English took under his command eleven tanks which fought an intense battle around the Montrabeau Woods and nearly fought their way into the small town of Exermont. Once again, Captain English was proving to be one of the 304th Tank Brigade's best junior leaders.

As the battle reached into 30 September, the 1st Corps issued an order to withdraw all tanks to reserve position for repairs, refueling, and general reorganization. The tanks and the soldiers of the 304th Tank Brigade earned a brief respite from the operation as they rested around the vicinity of Montblainville, Baulny, and Charpentry. However, the rest was short lived. As the Meuse-Argonne offensive neared its second week, twenty tanks were ordered to the 35th Infantry Division on 30 September. For once, the tanks saw little combat the last day of September.[29]

As the campaign entered October, the tanks again prepared for action. According to the after-action report, sixty-one tanks were ready for action on 1 October. However, while some eight tanks were ordered to cooperate with the 28th Infantry Division in attack, no major tank actions took place during the first three days of October. One of the main reasons was that the 304th Tank Brigade was nearing the point of exhaustion. The brigade suffered a terrible loss when Captain English, likely the best company commander in the brigade, was killed by German fire while leading his tanks on foot.[30]

To make matters worse, the great Spanish Flu of 1918 was beginning to seriously impact tank operations in the Meuse-Argonne; indeed, it affected not just the United States Tank Corps but both sides engaged in the war. As the brigade history commented, "The condition of the Brigade, by this time [5 October], was becoming very serious."[31] Soldiers of the 304th Tank Brigade stricken with the flu were evacuated, and this further sapped the brigade of manpower to operate the tanks. Furthermore, the flu meant there were fewer soldiers to repair the tanks.

Grappling with the depletion of the tanks, maintenance issues, and a lack of soldiers and officers fit for duty, Brigadier General Rockenbach took further action to return the tanks to some role in the offensive. On 11 October, Rockenbach ordered the creation of one Provisional Tank Company organized from the "remnants of the Brigade." Led by Captain Courtney Barnard and including nine other officers and 149 enlisted soldiers, the Provisional Company consisted of twenty-four tanks, a Dodge touring car, one motorcycle with sidecar, four trucks, one rolling kitchen, and a water cart.[32] After nearly two weeks of high-intensity conflict, overuse, and rough terrain, the American 304th Tank Brigade had been reduced from a brigade of almost 150 tanks to now just 24 tanks and a handful of men. The rest of the brigade, aside from the Provisional Company, was to return to Bourg and repair and refit for future operations.

After two days of reorganizing and readying the Provisional Tank Company, the mismatched unit received orders to shift to the 5th Army Corps's sector and attack with the 42nd Infantry Division between St. Georges and Landres on 15 October. However, one of Patton's great fears about tank employment nearly ruined the Provisional Tank Company before it reached the 42nd Division. As Patton and other tank officers had argued prior to both St. Mihiel and Meuse-Argonne, tanks could not traverse long distances by road. The shorter the ride from the railroad to the front, the better. However, as the Meuse-Argonne offensive approached nearly a month of continuous fighting, the infantry-heavy American First Army failed to understand the limitations of the Renault tanks. During the road march to the 42nd Infantry Division's sector, only ten American tanks were able to make it to the front lines. The rest of the tanks had broken down or were slowed by heavy traffic on the roads.[33] Despite a lack of support from division headquarters and above, the tanks were able to penetrate "deeply into the enemy's lines," but once again the infantry did not follow up, and the tanks were forced to fall back to Exermont.[34]

While the tiny Provisional Company proved to be a resilient force, the remnants of both the 344th and 345th Tank Battalions returned to Bourg, and those forces enjoyed relative rest until the end of the war. However, as the operation reached into November, the Provisional Tank Company saw limited action in the 2nd Infantry Division's attack between St. Georges and Landres on 1 November. While the tanks performed well according to the 2nd Infantry Division, by 2 November the remaining tanks and crews of the 304th Tank Brigade were beyond the point of exhaustion.[35] The brigade saw no more serious action in World War I following the end of the Meuse-Argonne offensive. The tanks, while a small part of the plan, had succeeded in proving their worth, but they had done so at quite a cost in manpower and materiel.

By 10 November the Meuse-Argonne offensive was over, and Patton was well on his way to recovering from his wound. Overall, the two battles of St. Mihiel and the Meuse-Argonne offensive cost the American Expeditionary Force over 129,000 casualties but inflicted nearly 150,000 casualties on the enemy while capturing 26,000 prisoners, 874 cannons, and 3,000 machine guns.[36] Regardless of the loss of life, the two battles helped push the Germans to the brink of defeat. As for Patton, the war was over, but he had earned his pay and learned numerous lessons that he would carry to World War II.

During the entirety of the Meuse-Argonne offensive, tanks and their crews from the 304th Tank Brigade went "over the top" eighteen times and the tanks were knocked out of action at a 123.4 percent rate.[37] The brigade earned numerous medals and awards, including two Medal of Honor winners. Corporal Donald M. Call received his Medal of Honor for conspicuous courage displayed on 26 September during the early phase of the Meuse-Argonne offensive when his tank was disabled and he carried his tank officer more than a mile to safety under heavy fire. Corporal Harold W. Roberts received his Medal of Honor posthumously. When his tank fell in the Aire River and flooded, Roberts told his driver, "Well only one of us can get out, and out you go."[38] Roberts had enough time to push his driver out of the Renault tank but had no time himself to get out and quickly drowned.

Thirteen men of the 304th Tank Brigade would receive Distinguished Service Crosses, including Patton and Major Sereno Brett as well as Captain Harry Semmes, Captain Math L. English, and Captain Julian K. Morrison. Officers from Patton's brigade received many medals, which showed that Patton's aggressive leadership style had paid dividends. From 26 September to 10 November, the 304th Tank Brigade suffered 170 casualties (2 officers killed, 21 wounded, 16 enlisted men killed, 131 wounded). Percentagewise, 5.34 percent of the 304th Tank Brigade officers were killed and 37.5 percent wounded. On the enlisted side of the brigade, 2.33 percent of the men were killed, while 18.8 percent were wounded.[39] As for the tanks, during the Meuse-Argonne the 304th Tank Brigade used roughly 150 tanks, and 174 tanks were repaired. Eighteen tanks were completely destroyed by enemy fire, roughly 12 percent of tanks in action. Only one tank was missing, and it was later found.[40]

Overall, the 304th Tank Brigade fought alongside the 4th Army

Corps, the 1st Infantry Division, and the 42nd Infantry Division during the St. Mihiel operation and served with the 1st Army Corps, the 5th Army Corps, and the 1st, 2nd, 28th, 42nd, 77th, 82nd, and 91st Infantry Divisions during the Meuse-Argonne offensive.[41] Despite being piecemealed out to numerous units, the 304th Tank Brigade earned an excellent reputation. As Patton lay wounded in his hospital bed, he wrote to his dear friend Sereno Brett, who commanded the brigade following Patton's wounding:

> I consider the enviable record of the 1st Brigade, Tank Corps, both in peace or war, had been due more to your earnest and constant efforts in training and valorous conduct in battle than to that of any other man or officer. . . . Not only did you work here when we had nothing, not even hope, without a murmur, but, in battle you fought the Brigade until there was nothing left and even after that, you fought on. . . . As far as I know no officer of the A.E.F. has given more faithful, loyal, and gallant service.[42]

While Patton and the Tank Corps believed the tanks had performed well, there was little evidence as to what impact the tanks had on the enemy. Judging from a series of articles clipped from German newspapers, captured documents, and prisoner-of-war statements, gathered by the Tank Corps in the years after the war,[43] the German High Command at first viewed tanks as rather barbaric and referred to the use of tanks in a tone similar to the Allied newspapers' when they lambasted the role of German gas and chemical weapons in the war. When Allied tanks first appeared, the Germans disregarded much of their potential. During the Battle of the Somme the Germans believed the tanks were not a long-term threat. However, on 9 April 1917, following the Battle of Arras, their views on tanks changed radically. In German reports, the Allies found evidence that for the first time the Germans realized they needed to change how they defended against tanks and called for "some special means of defence." General Erich Ludendorff issued an order after the Battle of Arras: "We will surely succeed in protecting ourselves against Tanks with these measures of defense [Artillery], but it is particularly important to combat in due time the great moral effect that Tanks have caused." From this point on, it was often found that German infantry would withdraw from tanks and leave it to the artillery to slow or destroy the tanks.

The great tank battle of Cambrai forced the Germans to fully realize that tanks were going to seriously harm their chances of victory. German general Georg von der Marwitz wrote following Cambrai, "By the use of innumerable Tanks the enemy have gained a victory near Cambrai." After the Russian withdrawal from the war, Field Marshal Paul von Hindenburg, who had yet to face tanks, did not put much stock in their use. By the middle of July, following the Battle of Soissons, the Germans admitted internally that tanks had "enormous possibilities." And at the end of July, General Ludendorff, who while a subordinate to Hindenburg was the leader of the German Army, issued an order stating: "The utmost attention must be paid to combating Tanks. Our earlier successes against Tanks have led to a certain contempt of this weapon of warfare. We must, however, now recken [sic] with more strongly armoured small, and more mobile Tanks which are more dangerous."

While the tanks and tankers of Patton's brigade were few in number, the role of tanks in World War I was clear: they helped the Allies win the war, lowered the morale of the enemy, and showed that with better production they could be an even stronger weapon system in future conflicts. For Patton, that fight was yet to come—first he had to recover—but his role in World War I was not quite over. As he lay in the hospital, he had plenty of time to write, to reflect on his experiences in both Mexico and France, and to ponder the future of tanks and his career.

6

The Spoils of War

Rest, Recovery, and Peace

(10 October 1918–17 March 1919)

> I'm damned sorry to see you leave the 1st Brigade, but happy to
> the same degree that you received a well-earned promotion.
> —Salerno Brett to Patton, 23 October 1918

As the Meuse-Argonne offensive raged on, Patton was stuck in the hospital recovering from his wound and writing many letters to his family as well as entries in his diary. After being wounded, Patton had first been evacuated to a temporary hospital just behind the front lines and stayed there until 29 September. From there he was moved to Base Hospital No. 49, where he continued to improve but also continued to complain about the speed of his recovery and his conditions. Patton wrote several letters going into great detail about his wound. To Beatrice he wrote, "The hole in my hip is about as big as a tea cup and they have to leave it open," and commented that he looked "as if I had just had a baby or was unwell. Still we broke the Prussian guard with the tanks so it is all fine. This is a stupid letter but it is hard to write."[1]

Patton initially expected a quick recovery, but although he was improving, the doctors were reluctant to move him out of the hospital until his wound had healed, especially when the Spanish Flu and various other seasonal illnesses were rampant. Patton's wound festered and frustrated him, mainly because he wanted to return to duty and get back in the fight. He did maintain a sense of humor about the wound, writing, "My scar wont show unless the styles change. I surely am a lucky fellow."[2]

A few days after being wounded, Patton was quite proud to read newspaper accounts of his exploits. The headline of one story read: "Col. Patton, Hero of Tanks, Hit by Bullet—Crawled into Shell Hole and Directed Monsters in Argonne Battle."[3] The article written by Thomas M. Johnson of the *Evening Sun* back home in California wrote of Patton's wounding: "As Patten [sic] walked forward a bullet struck him in the right leg. He walked about forty yards further, and then crawled into a shell hole. His orderly, Joseph Angelo of New York, bandaged the wound, whereupon Col. Patten lighted a cigarette and remained in the shell hole for some time, issuing orders to the tanks to spread out so as not to make so large a target."[4]

Patton also spent time reflecting on the service of the 304th Tank Brigade and was unreservedly proud of how his unit was fighting in the Meuse-Argonne and how it fought at St. Mihiel. He bragged to his wife: "I had seven Captains two majors and my self in the fight of these all are hit but one capt and the two majors. One Capt. Capt. English was killed and Capt. Higgins got both eyes shot out. Two Lts. Were killed and 15 wounded. But the tank corps established its reputation for not giving ground. They only went forward. And they are the only troops in the attack of whom that can be said."[5]

His 10 October letter to his wife is also telling, because it is the first time he begins to discuss what medal he will receive, or hopes to receive, for his service and his wounding. Initially Patton was desperate to get the Medal of Honor. "Perhaps I was mistaken but any way I believe I have been sited for decoration either the Medal of Honor or the military cross. I hope I get one of them."[6] In the meantime, while the Meuse-Argonne offensive was still raging and his unit was still very much in the fight, Patton received word that his boss, Brigadier General Rockenbach, had recommended him for promotion to colonel. While elated, Patton was worried that more rank would mean less fighting. For the first time in his career, Patton was wary of rank![7] His unease did not last long, as he was promoted to colonel effective 17 October 1918.[8] Patton had risen from a senior first lieutenant who set sail for France in 1917 and now, less than two years later, was a colonel and a brigade commander. Patton joked with his wife in a letter, "What do you think of me. I just got my colonelcy over the wire and am not yet 33. That is not so bad is it?"[9] He was, however, a realist and did not expect to retain his rank once the war was over. He commented to his wife that "the slump will be all the greater back to a captain" and that despite the promotion he would prefer a great decoration.[10]

If Patton's rise through the ranks was healthy, his wound was still not healing, and by the middle of October he was beginning to lose his patience, not just with his wound, but also with his medical care. His wound was "full of bugs" and the surgeons refused to sew it up until it was clean. Around this time Patton admitted to cursing out the surgeon, though he realized it was not going to do any good for his wound or his reputation but only make matters worse. Perhaps his anger with the doctors and surgeons stemmed from a comment made to Patton while in his hospital bed: around this time, a row of doctors remarked to their disgruntled patient that he looked forty-five years old. On 19 October, Patton admitted to his wife that he was looking older and in rough shape. He believed his aged appearance was due more to not being able to shave, and to having lost quite a bit of weight recovering from his injury, but it clearly was a sore subject and something he would seek to remedy once he was back on his feet.

While in the hospital Patton was buoyed by visits from friends and fellow officers alike. Patton wrote of a humorous meeting with French colonel Koechlin-Schwartz, who told Patton, "My dear Patton I am so glad you were wounded. For when you left I said to my wife that is the end of Patton he is one of those gallant fellows who always gets killed."[11] For Patton, it was likely the French colonel's comments figured as one of the greatest compliments of his life.

With little else to do, Patton began, as he had in the summer of 1917, to pine for the wife he had hardly seen since 1916. As friends came to visit Patton, he constantly asked how Beatrice Patton was doing and asked many of his good friends how she was looking. As he had done in 1917, Patton obsessed about his wife's appearance and was worried she had aged in his absence. He was preoccupied, more than usual, with making sure his wife did not have any gray hair and expressed the hope that if she did, she would dye her hair to remove the gray. He went so far to write to her about her appearance on 20 October: "I hope you will also your chin [sic]. I always think of you as Undine so I don't want you to look 33, even if I do."[12] There is no recorded response to this letter, but it is likely it was not well received by Beatrice, who by all indications was in perfectly good health and appearance.

On 25 October, Patton finally left the hospital and slowly moved back to Bourg to get back to work with the 304th Tank Brigade. Upon arrival, Patton discovered the Spanish Flu was spreading and causing increasing panic. While Patton was personally not worried about the flu, he was worried about the rather lax standards that had developed among the soldiers in his brigade. As he would do in World War II, and had done upon taking command of the 304th Tank Brigade earlier in the year, Patton set out to remedy the lack of discipline. One of his first acts upon returning to duty was to issue General Order No. 2 for the 302d Tank Center. He focused on proper haircuts, hair styles, and of course saluting:

4. Officers and men will shave daily and will see that their hair is kept short. Not clipped, but kept short, so that they look like soldiers not like poets or piano players.

5. The officers on duty with this Brigade have been cautioned as to exactness and smartness in saluting both officers and soldiers, and in the payment of other military and social courtesies which are founded on custom of the service and gentlemanly deportment.

6. There is a widespread and regrettable habit in our service of ducking the head to meet the hand in rendering a salute. This will not be tolerated.[13]

The focus on military standards is not unique to Patton or the times; however, it is important to note that Patton had written numerous memos on proper conduct and stressed its importance more than most officers. For Patton and his unit, discipline would be harder to enforce, as on 11 November 1918, the armistice was signed ending World War I. Patton had little to say about the end of the war, and perhaps there was a bit of sadness that the adventure was over and he would have to wait for the next big conflict for more military honor and glory. He wrote a brief diary entry on 11 November: "Peace was signed and Langres was very excited. Many flags. Got rid of my bandage. Wrote a poem on peace. Also one on Capt. English."[14]

The war is over and we pass
To pleasure after pain
Except those few who n'er shall see
Their native land again.

To one of these my memory turns
Noblest of noble slain
To Captain English of the Tanks
Who never shall return.

Yet should some future war exact
Of me the final debt
My fondest wish would be to tread
The path which he has set.

For faithful unto God and man

And to his duty true
He died to live for ever
In the hearts of those he knew.

Death found in him no faltering
But faithful to the last
He smiled into the face of fate
And mocked him as he passed.

No death to him was not defeat
But victory sublime
The grave promoted him to be
A hero for all time.[15]

It is important to note that at the time when the armistice was signed, no one knew the war would not start up again. The armistice eventually led to the Versailles Peace Treaty in 1919, but after the armistice was signed, units on both sides of the war had be to prepared for more fighting. By the end of 1918 the German Army was still an organized fighting force, and the war could easily have kicked off once again. As the interwar period would show and the rise of Hitler would make apparent, the German Army was not defeated but was still a viable fighting force at the time of the armistice.

While reimposing discipline, Patton, mainly to prevent boredom, decided to write and aimed to publish a book on his experience in World War I and on the birth of the United States Tank Corps. This was likely Patton's long-term aim once he got command of the 304th Tank Brigade, but on 16 November he wrote his wife to explain his reasons for writing the book:

To avoid so far as possible the devil of idleness I am going to write a book. For in prose it is the pen which makes the sword great in peace. So if I write a good book I might get to be a general before the next war now. If I start the next as a Brig. Gen. and hit the same pace I gained in this I will make three grades or end up as a full general. This is necessary to keep pace with [my sister] Nita. Or at least her present hopes.[16]

Patton would never publish a book on his role in the Great War; however, he and Brett, and possibly other officers around him, wrote a short history of the 304th Tank Brigade. The result reads less like a book and more like an after-action report of the brigade's performance in the war. It sticks to the facts and focuses almost entirely on the St. Mihiel operation and the Meuse-Argonne offensive. There is little commentary or analysis on how the brigade and the tanks performed. Patton did complete the draft and sent it to Rockenbach, who enjoyed the write-up and made some small comments for clarification and fact checking, but the report was never published. Patton never mentioned why not, and there is no evidence that he even tried to send it to publishers. If he did, it would likely have been accepted, as Americans wanted to read about the war, and also wanted to learn about one of the most famous new weapons in warfare.

The report is well written and clear. It is a very good read not just for experts but for those without much knowledge of World War I and tanks. Patton likely wrote the bulk of it, but Brett and others added the finishing touches and helped edit the report, and it is free of spelling errors, which means Patton did not write it without help. While Patton worked on the report, his focus quickly shifted to getting awards for not just his performance in the war but his wounding in the early hours of the Meuse-Argonne offensive.

Thrilled with what he had done so far, Patton was nevertheless slightly depressed by late November. While he had served his country and himself proudly, he still wanted to lead his tanks and unit into combat. "I feel terribly to have missed all the fighting."[17] Both bored with the war being over and frustrated by not being able to fight, Patton was growing restless, and not even his promotion to colonel helped his mood. Beyond his new rank, Patton had his eyes on greater glory for himself, and he was more desirous of getting the Distinguished Service Cross or hopefully the Medal of Honor. He even wrote, in the same letter announcing his colonelcy, "I do hope I get the decoration I would prefer it to the promotion."[18]

Almost immediately upon waking up in the hospital and realizing he was going to survive the war, Patton became set on getting as many medals and honors as he could. He would believe for the remainder of his life that he should have received a Medal of Honor for his actions on the day of his wounding. After realizing his actions and wounding might fall short of that honor, he shifted his attention to getting a Distinguished Service Cross. In World War I, and to this day, the Distinguished Service Cross is the second highest medal for extreme gallantry and risking one's life in service. It is similar to the Distinguished Service Medal, but that award can be given to officers and soldiers outside of combat, while the Distinguished Service Cross can only be awarded for combat action. Unlike the Medal of Honor, it does not bring with it extra pay or benefits, but is a rare honor to receive, and Patton should have been more than appreciative of such a singular award. Unfortunately, as he was prone to be, Patton was solely focused on the awards for personal gain and career advancement. To be sure, Patton was not alone in wanting ribbons and medals to further a career, but his letters home show how extreme his views were on the subject. On 18 November, Patton wrote his wife a rant-filled letter upon learning he was not going to get the Distinguished Service Cross. "The most terrible thing has happened to me. I heard last night that I will not get the D.S.C."[19] He added in anger: "I cannot realize it yet. It was the whole war to me. All I can ever get out of two years away from you . . . But I will get a G.D. if I am beat yet. I don't know what I will do but I will do something. If not I will resign and join the French army as a Captain or something. Gen. R. thinks my colonelcy is a compensation but it is nothing. I would rather be a second Lt. with D.S.C. than a general with out it."[20]

Martin Blumenson believed that Patton did not actively seek the Medal of Honor. While that is mostly true, Patton still wanted the Medal of Honor and harbored a hope for it, but as Blumenson wrote of this period, drawing an analogy with Patton's cadet days at West Point when he sought the office not of First Captain but of Adjutant, "It was as though some innate sense of inferiority prevented him from seeking the highest place."[21] Patton did discuss ways to get the Medal of Honor with friends and officers he trusted. Regardless of his reasons for pushing for the Medal of Honor of the Distinguished Service Cross, Patton was eventually awarded the Distinguished Service Cross and later the Distinguished Service Medal and wore them with pride the remainder of his life. As for the Medal of Honor, the last Patton wrote of it was a quick line in his diary stating simply: "I hope I get it."[22]

While his wound improved, Patton not only wrote letters to family and friends but also managed to write a few papers on his experience and the use of tanks. In early November he drew up a lecture titled "Practical Training, Tank Platoon," which discussed the operations and duties of tanks. "Tanks must watch their infantry. If the latter is held up there is a reason; the tanks must go back and find out. They must also always watch for helmet and rifle signals from the infantry. It is perfectly useless for tanks to attack more than 200 meters ahead of the Infantry. Tanks can take almost anything but they can hold practically nothing. Hence they *MUST STAY WITH THE INFANTRY.*"[23]

With the war over, Patton wrote quite a bit and tinkered with ideas about tanks in World War I and, now, in future wars. In his after-action report he drew nine tactical conclusions from his experience.

1. Infantry officers lacked understanding and appreciation of tank capabilities, for tanks needed infantry operating with them at all times to be successful.
2. A lack of liaison between tanks and infantry hampered efficient operations.
3. Infantry should act as though tanks were not present and not expect tanks to overcome resistance and wait expecting tanks to attempt to consolidate a success.
4. Tanks were too valuable because of their strengths in firepower and mobility and too weak in mechanical reliability to be dissipated in reconnaissance missions.
5. The distance between readiness positions and the line of departure should be reduced, for tanks "cannot sustain a prolonged march without being overhauled and put in order."
6. A thorough preliminary reconnaissance on foot of the terrain to be used by tanks was absolutely indispensable.
7. The enemy artillery is the dangerous adversary of the tanks." Therefore, strong supporting artillery ready to deliver counter-battery fires, as well as screening smoke, was terribly important to insure tank success.
8. The value of tanks as attacking units and as a fighting arm had been demonstrated.
9. Some slight changes in tactical employment were necessary, those looking forward toward a better utilization of tanks in mass and in depth.[24]

This report further showed the development of Patton's writing skill and of his ideas on tanks and tank warfare. Although Patton would leave tanks after the war and fail to revolutionize and develop blitzkrieg tactics, his impact on the development of the United States Tank Corps was very substantial. While he kept busy with writing, Patton continued to focus on training his soldiers and readying the brigade for departure back to the United States.

On 4 December 1918, Patton finally received official word on his quest for the Distinguished Service Cross: he would indeed receive the award. What is surprising, instead of a long-winded, proud letter home or gloating diary entry, he marked the announcement in his diary by stating only, "Got D.S.C."[25] The official citation read: "For extraordinary heroism in action near Cheppy, France, September 26, 1918. He displayed conspicuous courage, coolness, energy, and intelligence in directing the advance of his brigade down the valley of the Aire. Later he rallied a force of disorganized infantry and led it forward behind the tanks under heavy machine-gun and artillery fire until he was wounded. Unable to advance any further, he continued to direct the operations of his unit until all arrangements for turning over the command were completed."[26]

A few days later, perhaps to celebrate, Patton purchased his first "war" dog, a German Shepherd named Char, for $200. He wrote to his wife about the purchase, "Since marrying you I have never been satisfied with any thing but the best even in dogs."[27] Just as he had at the beginning of his service overseas with the purchase of a very expensive vehicle, Patton made good use of his wife's wealth to purchase Char, for what today would be equivalent to slightly more than $3,000.

Patton received congratulations from friends, family members, and fellow officers on the Distinguished Service Cross, but likely the highest praise came from his wife. In one of the few letters that remain from Beatrice Patton, she wrote her husband after she received confirmation of his award, "Georgie, you are the fulfillment of all the ideals of manliness and high courage & bravery I have always held for you, ever since I have known you. And I have expected more of you than any one else in the world ever has or will."[28] It is likely this letter was saved by Patton and his family for the simple reason that it shows that, while they had been apart for more than two years, the love and bond between the two was still remarkably strong.

As 1919 began, Patton began to refocus his attention on getting back home to his wife and children. War, however, was never far from his mind, and as early as January 1919 he started to plan for the next great war. Patton wrote a letter to his father that further shows why Patton wanted another war, and it was mainly for selfish reasons: "I think that in six months we will have to go to Russia for a war. So I hope I can get back for a little while any way. Them I must come back so as to get the medal of Honor, which I missed getting this time on account of all the witness getting killed or being Bosch."[29]

Patton even prior to World War I assumed the next great war would be fought in Mexico. In 1919 that idea was not novel or really surprising.

The recent Mexican Punitive Expedition was still in Patton's mind, and the belief was that they had not quite completed their mission, as Pancho Villa was still roaming Mexico and the Mexican government was still in turmoil. Yet Patton was also not incorrect about war in Russia. In January 1919 the Russian Revolution was continuing, and a small American force would eventually be sent to participate in the war. Patton, however, was not going to be one of the officers to go, and by 1919 he knew it was time to head back home.

During the month of January 1919, Patton kept busy with writing, training, and lecturing army officers about tanks and tank warfare. At this point Patton had developed an excellent reputation for his lectures and enjoyed talking to his fellow officers and to senior officers. Along with lecturing, he gave numerous tank demonstrations to officers, many of whom had never seen tanks, let alone seen them in action.

By February, Patton's attention turned toward the long engagement and relationship between his sister Nita and the great hero of the day, General John J. Pershing. In 1916 and 1917, Pershing and Nita Patton had developed a relationship and were engaged to marry. For Patton, it was a double-edged sword. While he viewed Pershing as a mentor and in many ways modeled his behavior and military bearing after Pershing, Patton also was wary of favoritism. When Patton arrived in France with Pershing in 1917, his sister's relationship with Pershing was not in doubt, and Patton wrote extensively to his wife and talked personally with Pershing often about Nita and their marriage plans. However, as the war dragged on and Pershing's responsibilities grew, it seemed his engagement with Nita Patton might not last beyond the war. To make matters worse for Nita Patton, rumors had spread across the Atlantic that Pershing had taken a young Frenchwoman as his mistress. By February 1919, with the war over, Patton had more time on his hands and, as he had shown in 1917, was more than willing to gossip about his sister's relationship with his boss. He wrote to Beatrice, "As to J. and Nita. It is possible that the game is up. You see he could get anyone in the world and they are after him. Ambition is a great thing and without soul."[30] Patton wrote a few days later in more detail: "Nita loves him and he her (or she) it might be unpleasant for her to come but it would be more unpleasant for her to loose him. He is great and much sought after one more year of separation might ruin two lives and loves. It is better for her pride to suffer a little than for her to loose such a Great man. Therefore I say tell her to come. One word from her and he can fix it."[31]

By February 1919 their engagement was over. Pershing would remain a widower until he married in secret soon before his death, and Nita would never marry. Despite a few attempts at reconciliation, Nita Patton, a strong and intelligent woman, rebuffed Pershing at every attempt. The two remained distant for the remainder of their lives, and their relationship never recovered. As for Patton, he was relieved that it was over and he could continue his career without the cloud of favoritism.

As spring slowly returned to France and the farmers of Europe reclaimed the battle-torn land, Patton finally prepared to return to the United States. Prior to leaving, Patton thanked his soldiers and particularly General Pershing, "I have attempted in a small way to model my self on you and what ever success I have had has been due to you as an inspiration."[32] With goodbyes said, Patton left aboard the SS *Patria* on March 1 and arrived in New York to much fanfare on 17 March 1919. Swarmed by newspaper reporters, Patton was quoted in the *New York Evening Mail* as saying, "The tank is only used in extreme cases of stubborn resistance. They are the natural answer to the machine gun, and as far as welfare is concerned, have come to stay just as much as the airplanes have."[33] For Patton the war was over, but his role with tanks was not, and though there would be no machine guns and artillery fire, Patton and the rest of the United States Tank Corps readied for another fight, this time with the United States Army and the budget of the United States government.

7

The War after the War
The Fight for the United States Tank Corps
(18 March 1919–December 1921)

> For the present I shall stay in the Tank Corps as I will thus
> probably keep my rank and besides I owe it to the Corps.
> —Patton to George S. Patton Sr., 1 April 1919

Patton finally returned to the United States and his wife and two young children, whom he had rarely seen since 1916. Patton at the age of thirty-four was still a colonel and still a part of the United States Tank Corps. A battle was brewing within the United States Army, the War Department, and Congress about what to do with tanks and the air service. There was going to be a fight for the United States Tank Corps, but in the meantime Patton decided to stay with the tanks for the next couple of years, mainly out of loyalty. In April 1919, Patton wrote his dad confirming his resolve to stay in the Tank Corps for a while longer, as he thought he "owe[d] it to the Corps."[1] Toward the end of February 1919, Patton wrote a letter to General Rockenbach thanking him for his mentorship and help in the war, adding, "I want also to take this opportunity of saying good by and of expressing to you my sincere appreciation of all that you put up with from me. My excuse is the one you like best 'We put it over.'"[2] The two men were never close, but it is clear there was a level of respect and appreciation between them. Whether because of age, rank, or personality, the two did not bond personally, but they worked well together during the war. Years later, as Patton reached international fame, an older and still calm Rockenbach wrote Beatrice Patton an honest assessment of Patton and of their relationship during World War I:

> Patton had his chances and there is no other officer in the U.S.A. doing or capable of doing more with them. . . . He was, in my mind like a son and I did not spare him the rod in training him for the great things I believed him capable of. I remember warn-

ing him on the eve of St. Mihiel that he was in command of a brigade and that it was his duty to see that his supply of Gas, grease
and ammunition w/ was kept up. That there was no question of
his personal courage. That our objective was to kill Germans
and not get Killed or wounded. I saw from his expression that I
had not impressed him and I remarked I am serious if tomorrow
I find you in a tank, doing the work of a private, I will relieve
you. He remarked—If you find me in a tank. Next day he led
from the top of a tank his brigade in action. Brett who heard my
remark led his battalion on foot.[3]

Later in the letter, Rockenbach wrote a short story about Patton and
how, maybe, he had finally heeded the words of his old World War I
boss. Rockenbach quoted a now famous speech given by Patton in 1944
in which he told his unit, "An army is a team; it lives, sleeps, eats, fights
as a team. This individual heroic stuff is a lot of crap."[4] Perhaps, after
nearly thirty years, Patton learned that it was not the individual or the
commander that won wars, but a team, a unit of trained soldiers! Perhaps, out of all the lessons learned, this may have been the greatest lesson Patton learned in war, and in many ways he owed it to his old boss,
Brigadier General Sam Rockenbach.

On 22 April, Patton received his next assignment. As expected, he
was to remain with the Tank Corps, and along with a few other officers
he was tasked with compiling a manual on Tank Drill Regulation.[5] The
duty position was ideal for Patton for several reasons. One, he would
keep his rank as colonel for a while longer. Second, he was ordered to live
at Fort Meade, which both Patton and his wife approved of. And lastly,
he would get to have some input on the future of tanks in the United
States Army.

Before getting back into the life of a garrison officer, Patton had
to readjust to family life and, in many ways, reintroduce himself to his
children, especially his younger daughter. Ruth Ellen Patton Totten viv-
idly remembered seeing her dad for the first time after he returned from
France. To the three-year-old Ruth Ellie, he seemed:

an ogre. Everything I did was wrong. I will never forget the first
time he ever spoke directly to me. I had rushed into the house
not knowing he was there, and he was sitting on the living-room
floor among a lot of dismembered guns which he was cleaning
and re-assembling. He looked up at me as I hovered in the door-

way, and with his really charming smile said: "Hello, little girl."
I was so overwhelmed with the attention that I burst into tears
and howls, and he began to yell at Ma to "come and take the
baby away," that she was "making a goddam awful noise," and
that he hadn't touched her.[6]

For most soldiers returning from a long deployment, there is a period of
intense adjustment. Patton was no different, and he had basically been
deployed in combat since 1916. He, needless to say, had a tough time
readjusting to life with kids. Ruth Ellen wrote of the time:

> I realize now that he was in considerable pain at the time; wor-
> ried about his future in the tank corps of his creation; and having
> a hangover from the war, which is a very real thing. A man goes
> from the command of thousands of men where his judgement
> means victory or defeat, life or death, to the shrinking command
> of a handful of men, and the narrowing horizons of peacetime
> duty with not enough money and not enough troops, and the
> tender trap of home and family—and, it is a let-down. I guess
> things didn't come up to Georgie's expectations either.[7]

Patton would slowly win over Ruth Ellen and his older daughter Beatrice,
Little Bee for short. Historians often like to play psychologist, and that is
rather dangerous, but nearly every soldier has issues returning from combat to a home environment. For some it takes a lifetime to return to normal; the experience of war never goes away, it is always there. And for
family members, it is and will always be hard to understand. As for Ruth
Ellen, she never had a close relationship with her father as her sister did.
The Pattons finally got their son in 1923 when George S. Patton IV was
born. George IV would eventually rise to the rank of major general and
was considered by Martin Blumenson to be one of the greatest field commanders in military history.

As Patton worked on the regulation manual for tanks, he began to
ready his next career move. The question in Patton's mind was, should he
stay with the Tank Corps or return to his commissioning branch, the cavalry. At first, in the spring of 1919, Patton was high on the future of the
United States Tank Corps, as he wrote, "That stateus of the T.C. is very
bright here in fact I think that we are in the best position of any corps in
the army."[8] However, as the financial debate began in Congress and the
United States Army began to return to prewar size, the Versailles Peace

Treaty was signed officially ending World War I. Patton decided it was in his best interests personally and professionally to return to the cavalry. He stubbornly, but likely correctly, clung to his old belief that the cavalry offered better promotion chances. By the end of the summer in 1919, Patton had all but made up his mind when he wrote Rockenbach that he was likely going to leave the Tank Corps:

> When I returned from leave last September you asked me if, 'I was like the rest of them hunting for a soft billet and leaving the Tank Corps.' I told you that while I did not intend to remain in the Tank Corps I was prepared to stay in it for another year and do my best to reorganise. I have done my best and the year is up.
>
> In justice of my self I do not believe that to stay longer would be wise. The cavalry is now being reorganised and if I am to get on in it I should be back with it. Further I believe that the next war will be with Mexico and that in such a war tanks will be of no practical use. Of course I would not mention this belief to any one else.[9]

By 1920, as the United States Army and Patton returned to a peace-time footing and garrison duty, Patton was reduced to his last permanent rank, his prewar rank of captain. However, with his service record and his closeness to General Pershing working in his favor, Patton was one of the lucky few to be quickly promoted to major, effective 1 July 1920. Prior to being promoted, Patton, as he was prone to do on a yearly basis, injured himself riding his horse. Happily, he escaped severe injury. The medical report stated: "While riding horse on target-range, Tank Corps, Camp Meade, Md., December 22, 1919, the animal 'bucked,' and the officer was thrown forward on the pommel of the saddle and sustained injuries to his testicles."[10] There is no specific evidence, since his brain was never collected for study, but Patton had numerous head injuries throughout his life and likely suffered numerous moderate to severe concussions. During World War I alone he was thrown out of his automobile and suffered numerous bumps, bruises, and cuts, and prior to that he sustained serious injuries in falls playing polo and in other car accidents. Based on current head trauma science, it is possible that as Patton aged he was suffering from chronic traumatic encephalopathy, or CTE. Chronic traumatic encephalopathy is a degenerative brain disease found in athletes, mainly football players but also athletes from other sports such as soccer, in military veterans, and in others with a history of repetitive brain trauma. Without a study of Patton's brain there is no way to fully know if he suffered from CTE, but it is an area that needs further study and could partially explain his increasingly angry outbursts and bizarre statements made during the latter stages of World War II. Martin Blumenson toward the end of his life believed the constant head injuries had to have played a part in his behavior, not just in World War II but during the interwar period as he became more subject to mood swings and depression.

By the summer of 1920, Patton was ready to leave the Tank Corps, and after his promotion to major in August, he was officially relieved of command of the 304th Tank Brigade on 4 September 1920. Patton returned to his old service and reported to the 3d Cavalry Regiment at Fort Myer. With his return to the cavalry branch, Patton's World War I career ended and he entered the next stage of his life and career, readying himself for the next war. While he was no longer a tanker, he would continue to think and write about the future of tanks.

As he had shown throughout his life, Patton was a writer, and he published on tanks for a couple of years following the end of World War I. Even as a cavalry officer, Patton still thought about tanks and imagined the role of tanks in future wars. Unlike some officers who stayed in the Tank Corps, Patton was not a religious zealot about tanks. Mainly he wanted to be promoted, and the United States Army has a checkered past that continues to this day on how it treats prolific writers. Some gain fame and rank, while others, such as Billy Mitchell in World War I and Jim Gant in the current war in Afghanistan, get in trouble and are removed from the army. Patton's interwar writings were always guarded, and purposely so.

In May 1920, while still a colonel, Patton wrote a short article titled "Tanks in Future Wars" for the United States Army's *Infantry Journal*. The article is not groundbreaking or remotely radical, but it does offer a sound and realistic view of tanks in the era in which Patton was writing. Following the end of World War I, the American Expeditionary Force was no more, and the United States Army was returning to its tiny pre-war levels. For Patton personally, that meant a reduction in rank and responsibility, but he understood that tanks would be a weapon system in some possible war. In directing his article toward the infantry, Patton wrote, "My purpose is simply to call their attention to what appears to be a lack of effort in that direction, to show some of the causes which have led to this lassitude, and to suggest, in a very sketchy manner, certain tactical uses to which tanks will be set in future wars."[11] Patton realized, and had argued during the war, that a vast majority of the United States Army had little to no concept about tanks and how they operate, and during the interwar period he worked to fix that issue. In a rather humorous way, Patton outlined how most in the army viewed tanks: "Only those of us who doctored and nursed the grotesque war-babies of 1918 through innumerable inherent ills of premature birth know how bad they really were, and, by virtue of that same intimate association, are capable of judging how much better they are now and how surely they will continue to improve."[12] He later added: "To the casual observer, the tank of 1918 is the last word. It is the tank, a feeble, blind, lumbering affair, 'half devil and half child.'"[13]

"Tanks in Future Wars" is a defense of tanks, but the only remark Patton makes in the entire article that could be deemed radical is at the very end when he predicts, rather accurately, the elevation of the United States Tank Corps to an independent branch: "Like the air service, they are destined for a separate existence."[14] Patton was not arguing for a separate branch of the military akin to the Marine Corps or the eventual Air Force, but as he had argued during the war, he wanted an independent tank corps, equivalent to the artillery and infantry branches of the United States Army.

A year later, Patton was involved in professional and intellectual debate about the roles of tanks and about the tank corps being an independent branch of the United States Army. In July 1921, Patton along with Major Bradford C. Chynoweth published a two-page exchange titled "Comments on 'Cavalry Tanks'" in the *Journal of the United States Cavalry Association*. Chynoweth advocated for tanks but argued that tanks should be part of the Cavalry Corps. Patton responded with the shortcomings of tanks and why they could not serve in the cavalry: "I was, and believe that I still am as enthusiastic a tanker as ever caterpillared, yet I cannot bring myself to the point of picturing tanks, in the mountains of Mexico, the rice paddies of the Philippines, the forests of Canada, or, in face of competent artillery, on the sandy and gully-infested plains of Texas."[15]

Patton, who during this time believed the next war would be in Mexico, doubted the usefulness of tanks in that terrain. However, while Patton disagreed with Chynoweth's thesis, he maintained, as he wrote in 1920, that the United States Tank Corps should be independent. "What is wanted, then, is neither infantry tanks nor cavalry tanks, but a Tank Corps—a special mobile general headquarters reserve, to be detailed, as circumstances demand, with whichever arm it can best co-operate."[16]

Through the end of 1921, Patton still read and discussed updated tank doctrine, but eventually he returned to the traditional duties of a major in the United States Army. He completed each job with gusto and proved his value at every command. He still dreamt of the next big war and what his role would be. By the time World War II started in 1939, Patton, while no longer a first lieutenant, was again was not in the position he desired. Eventually, however, he would see his dreams fulfilled and the legend of Patton would rise anew in World War II. For that, he can thank the birth of the United States Tank Corps and his role in World War I.

Conclusion

The principles of the art of war are unchangeable. The man of vision, the inventor of war machines who does not keep this in mind and does not study the fitting of his instrument into the army organization so that it will assist and not disrupt gets a quick shift.

—Samuel Rockenbach, "The Tank Corps of the American Expeditionary Force"

Prior to the Great War, George S. Patton was a lowly lieutenant known more for his personal wealth than his military ability. World War I changed all that. Always a driven and intrepid soldier, Patton was a decent peacetime officer, but in peace he had no chance to succeed, or to rise through the ranks. World War I offered Patton a chance to prove his abilities to his superiors, his family, and, more important, himself. The war taught Patton how to organize, how to command, and how to lead men in battle and make them do things they did not want to do. As he reflected on his command while recovering from his wound in October 1918, he wrote: "Now I know that I could command a Division. Things really are much easier than they appear."[1] Without his experience in World War I, Patton would never have learned how to prepare and lead men for war, and without this knowledge there would have been no dashing Third Army commander to help win World War II.

The importance of World War I for Patton's career cannot be overstated. Arriving in Paris as a staff officer to Pershing, Patton left the war a decorated hero with the rank of colonel. During his two years in Europe, Patton met many of the leaders of World War II, including George C. Marshall who believed that Patton was still young enough to lead Americans into battle by 1942. It was Patton's age when the Second World War started that concerned him the most. He feared he was perceived as too old, and that partially explains his rough and outrageous personality. It was a disguise to trick others into believing he was young and fit enough for the next big fight. Patton did not know at the time, but he did not need to trick anyone, least of all Marshall and Eisenhower. Throughout his experiences in Mexico and France, Patton's relationship with Pershing proved invaluable to his career as he moved from good job to good job. While the interwar years were hard for Patton personally and for his family, his career never really suffered. The period between the wars was tough on the United States Army, the budget, and the soldiers, but Patton was able to keep his career on track, and when Hitler and the German Army attacked Poland, Patton was in a great position to earn an important role in the war.

As for his beloved tanks, the Tank Corps was eventually disbanded after the passage of the National Defense Act of 1920, and not until war clouds swept across Europe did it return.[2] When World War II started, Patton was called on almost immediately to lead tanks into battle. Once again, when given the chance, Patton succeeded. From victory in Sicily with the Seventh Army to his masterful job with the Third Army, Patton deserves a special place in the history of America and the United States Army. As the first tanker in United States history, the legend of Patton was born in World War I, and it was his experience in that war that shaped and molded what he was to become and do in World War II.

Acknowledgments

This book would have been impossible to write without the support of my colleagues on Team 29 at Fort Belvoir. Special thanks go to Colonel David Haught (Ret), Colonel Mark Hurley (Ret), and Colonel Zsolt Szentkiralyi (Ret) for their patience through the process of researching and writing and for their time reading drafts of the manuscript. I would like to thank my family and friends for their love and support throughout my life and the writing of this book. To my wonderful wife, "You can do it!"

Appendix A
Order of Battle, St. Mihiel and Meuse-Argonne

Order of Battle (Allied Powers)

Allied Armies:
  Marshal Ferdinand Foch, Commanding
  General Maxime Weygand, Chief of Staff
Armies of the North and Northeast:
  General Philippe Pétain, Commanding
  General Edmond Buat, Chief of Staff
American General Headquarters:
  General John J. Pershing, Commanding
  Maj. Gen. James W. McAndrew, Chief of Staff
American First Army:
  General John J. Pershing, Commanding
  Col. Hugh A. Drum, Chief of Staff
Group of Armies of the Center:
  General Paul André Maistre, Commanding
  General René Mollandin, Chief of Staff
Group of Armies of the Reserve:
  General Marie Émile Fayolle, Commanding
  General Gabriel Alexandre Paquette, Chief of Staff
French Tenth Army:
  General Joseph Mangin, Commanding
  Col. Émile Hergault, Chief of Staff
French I Corps:
  General Gustave Paul Lacapelle, Commanding
  French 153d Division
  French 69th Division
French XX Corps:
  General Pierre Berdoulat, Commanding
  American 1st Division

Moroccan 1st Division
American 2d Division
American III Corps* (in reserve):
  Maj. Gen. Robert Lee Bullard, Commanding
  Brig. Gen. A. W. Bjornstadt, Chief of Staff
  *administrative control only of American units in French Tenth Army
French XXX Corps:
  General Hippolyte-Alphonse Pénet, Commanding
  French 38th Division
  French 48th Division
French XI Corps:
  General Marie Léon Louis Prax, Commanding
  French 128th Division
  French 41st Division
French Sixth Army:
  General Jean Marie Degoutte, Commanding
  Col. Georges Émile Brion, Chief of Staff
    French II Corps:
      General Edme Philipot, Commanding
      French 33d Division
      French 47th Division
      French 2d Division (plus 7th Infantry Brigade of American
        4th Division)
    French VII Corps:
      General André Massenet, Commanding
      French 164th Division (plus American 4th Division less 7th
        Infantry Brigade)
    American I Corps:
      Maj. Gen. Hunter Liggett, Commanding
      Brig. Gen. Malin Craig, Chief of Staff
      French 167th Division
French Ninth Army:
  General Antoine De Mitry, Commanding
  General Alexandre Peschart d'Ambly, Chief of Staff
    French XXXIV Corps:
      General Jean Frédéric Piarron de Mondésir, Commanding
      French 39th Division
      American 3d Division
    French III Corps:
      General Léonce Lebrun, Commanding

French 73d Division
French 4th Division
French 20th Division
French 18th Division
American 28th Division (in reserve)
French Fifth Army:
General Henri Berthelot, Commanding
Col. Charles Belhague, Chief of Staff
French I Cavalry Corps:
General Eugène Féraud, Commanding
French 77th Division
French 5th Division
French 131st Division
French 3d Division
French V Corps:
General Maurice Pellé, Commanding
French 10th Division
French 7th Division
French 9th Division
French 40th Division
Italian II Corps
Colonial I Corps

Order of Battle of American Divisions

American 1st Division:
Maj. Gen. Charles P. Summerall, Commanding
Col. Campbell King, Chief of Staff
1st Infantry Brigade
2d Infantry Brigade
1st Field Artillery Brigade
French 42d Aero Squadron. Detached: 1st Sanitary Train
French 83d Balloon Company
French 253d Field Artillery truck-carried (75)
French 11th and 12th Groups of Tanks
American 2d Division:
Maj. Gen. James G. Harbord, Commanding
Col. Preston Brown, Chief of Staff
3d Infantry Brigade
4th Marine Brigade

2d Field Artillery Brigade
10 French airplanes
Artillery of French 58th Division
French 288th Field Artillery (75)
French 11th and 12th Groups Heavy Tanks
American 4th Division:
    Maj. Gen. George H. Cameron, Commanding
    Lt. Col. C. A. Bach, Chief of Staff
        7th Infantry Brigade
        8th Infantry Brigade
        4th Field Artillery Brigade
        51st Field Artillery Brigade
American 26th Division:
    Maj. Gen. Clarence R. Edwards, Commanding
    Col. Duncan K. Major, Chief of Staff
        51st Infantry Brigade
        52d Infantry Brigade
        51st Field Artillery Brigade
        56th Infantry Brigade
American 42d Division:
    Maj. Gen. Charles T. Menoher, Commanding
    Brig. Gen. Douglas MacArthur, Chief of Staff
        83d Infantry Brigade
        84th Infantry Brigade
        67th Field Artillery Brigade
American 3d Division:
    Maj. Gen. Joseph T. Dickman, Commanding
    Col. Fred. H. Turner, Chief of Staff
        5th Infantry Brigade
        6th Infantry Brigade
American 32d Division
    Maj. Gen. William G. Haan, Commanding
    Lt. Col. Robert McC. Beck Jr., Chief of Staff
        63d Infantry Brigade
        64th Infantry Brigade
        57th Field Artillery Brigade
        147th Field Artillery Brigade
        3d Field Artillery Brigade
American 28th Division:
    Maj. Gen. Charles H. Muir, Commanding

Brig. Gen. Edward L. King and Lt. Col. Joe R. Brabson, Chiefs of Staff
  3d Field Artillery Brigade
  3d Battalion, 18th Field Artillery
  55th Infantry Brigade
  56th Infantry Brigade
  53d Field Artillery Brigade

Appendix B

Order of Battle, 1st/304th Tank Brigade

United States Tank Corps:
> Brig. Gen. Samuel D. Rockenbach, Commanding
> Lt. Col. D. D. Pullen, Chief of Staff
>   1st Tank Brigade
>   Lt. Col. George S. Patton Jr., Commanding
>   326th/344th Tank Battalion*
>   Maj. Sereno E. Brett, Commanding
>   327th/345th Tank Battalion*
>   Capt. Ranulf Compton, Commanding
>   French XI Group (St. Chamond)
>   Chef de Bataillon Auguste Herlaut, Commanding
>   French XIV Group (Schneider)
>   Chef d'Escadrons C. M. M. Chanoine
>   3rd Tank Brigade (Headquarters only for liaison with French tanks)
>   Lt. Col. D. D. Pullen, Commanding
>   French Headquarters, Lt. Col. Émile Wahl, Commanding

*Patton and Compton Diary, 10, 12 September 1918: "General Order #16 General Headquarters Tank Corps this date changing designations of 326th and 327th Battalions to 344th and 345th Battalions respectively."

Appendix C

Allied Tanks of World War I

Note: All specifications are from the Samuel Rockenbach Papers at Virginia Military Institute, Lexington, Virginia.

French Renault Tank

Dimensions: length 13 feet 5½ inches, width 5 feet 8 inches, height
   7 feet 6 inches
Armor thickness: 6–16 millimeters
Weight: 7¼ tons
Engine: Renault four cylinder, 27 horsepower
Transmission: mechanical gear (four forward, one reverse)
Maximum speed: 5 miles per hour
Armament: one 37-millimeter tank cannon (male tanks); one .303
   Hotchkiss machine gun (female tanks)
Obstacle ability: could cross trenches 6 feet wide
Crew: two soldiers

French St. Chamond Tank

Dimensions: length 25 feet 11¾ inches, width 8 feet 9 inches, height
   7 feet 7 inches
Armor thickness: 6–16 millimeters
Weight: 23 tons
Engine: Panhard four cylinder, 92 horsepower
Transmission: electric (variable speeds)
Maximum speed: 7½ miles per hour
Armament: one 75-millimeter tank cannon and four machine guns
Obstacle ability: could cross trenches 8 feet wide
Crew: nine soldiers

French Schneider Tank

Dimensions: length 20 feet 4 inches, width 7 feet, height 7 feet 8½
   inches
Armor thickness: 6–16 millimeters
Weight: 15 tons
Engine: Schneider four cylinder, 60 horsepower
Transmission: mechanical gear (three gears)
Maximum speed: 4 miles per hour
Armament: one 75-millimeter tank cannon and two machine guns
Obstacle ability: could cross trenches 5 feet wide
Crew: six soldiers

British Mark V Tank

Dimensions: length 26 feet 5 inches, width 13 feet 9 inches, height
   9 feet
Armor thickness: 6–12 millimeters
Weight: 29 tons
Engine: Ricardo six cylinder, 150 horsepower
Transmission: mechanical gear (four speeds)
Maximum speed: 4½ miles per hour
Armament: two 6-pound guns and four machine guns (male tank);
   six machine guns (female tank)
Obstacle ability: could cross trenches 14 feet wide
Crew: eight soldiers

British Mark V Star Tank

Dimensions: length 32 feet 5 inches, width 13 feet 9 inches, height
   9 feet
Armor thickness: 6–12 millimeters
Weight: 32 tons
Engine: Ricardo six cylinder, 150 horsepower
Transmission: planetary gear (four speeds)
Maximum speed: 4 miles per hour
Armament: two 6-pound guns and four machine guns (male tank);
   six machine guns (female tank)
Obstacle ability: could cross trenches 16 feet wide
Crew: eight soldiers

Anglo-American Mark VII Tank (Secret)

Dimensions: length 34 feet 2½ inches, width 12 feet 8 inches, height 10 feet 3 inches

Armor thickness: 6–12 millimeters

Weight: 35 tons

Engine: Liberty twelve cylinder, 300 horsepower

Transmission: planetary gear (two forward, two reverse)

Maximum speed: 5¼ miles per hour

Armament: two 6-pound guns and four machine guns, or seven machine guns

Obstacle ability: could cross trenches 16 feet wide

Crew: ten soldiers, one officer

American Renault Tank

Dimensions: length 15 feet 7 inches, width 5 feet 9 inches, height 7 feet 6½ inches

Armor thickness: 3–16 millimeters

Weight: 6½ tons

Engine: Buda four cylinder, 40 horsepower

Transmission: mechanical gear (four forward, one reverse)

Maximum speed: 5 miles per hour

Armament: one 37-millimeter tank cannon (male tanks); one .30 Marlin machine gun (female tanks)

Obstacle ability: could cross trenches 7 feet wide

Crew: two soldiers

Appendix D

Patton Chronology

1885: Born 11 November in San Gabriel, California

1903–1904: Attends Virginia Military Institute, Lexington, Virginia

1904–1909: Attends United States Military Academy, West Point, New York

1909: Assigned to Fifteenth United States Cavalry upon graduation

1910: Marries Beatrice Ayer

1912: Finishes fifth in the modern pentathlon at the 1912 Summer Olympics in Stockholm

1916–1917: Aide-de-camp to General John J. Pershing, Mexican Punitive Expedition

1917: In France as aide-de-camp to General John J. Pershing, Commander in Chief, American Expeditionary Forces; commands Headquarters Troop, American Expeditionary Forces

1917–1918: Assigned as first member of United States Tank Corps, later serves as Commander, 304th Tank Brigade; wounded in combat; receives Distinguished Service Cross; promoted to temporary rank of colonel

1921–1922: Commander, First Squadron, Third United States Cavalry, Fort Myer, Virginia

1924–1928: Serves in various staff roles in Hawai'i

1932: Graduates from United States Army War College

1932–1935: Executive Officer, Third United States Cavalry, Fort Myer, Virginia

1935–1937: G-2, United States Army General Staff, Hawai'ian Department

1938–1940: Commander, Third United States Cavalry, Fort Myer, Virginia; promoted to brigadier general

1940: Commander, Second Armored Brigade, Second Armored Division, Fort Benning, Georgia

1941–1942: Commander, Second Armored Division, Fort Benning, Georgia; promoted to major general

1942: Commander, I Armored Corps, First and Second Armored Divisions

1942–1943: Commands Western Task Force during Allied landings and subsequent campaign in North Africa; promoted to lieutenant general

1943–1944: Resumes command of I Armored Corps in preparation for invasion of Sicily; commands Seventh United States Army during Operation Husky

1944–1945: Commander, Third United States Army; leads Third Army across France, Germany, Czechoslovakia, and Austria

1945: Commander, Fifteenth United States Army; dies 21 December in motor accident in Heidelberg, Germany

Notes

Where the name Patton appears alone, it is understood to mean George S. Patton Jr.

Introduction

Patton attributes the words of the epigraph to "an officer who had once been my troop commander" (*The Patton Papers*, 1:434), sometimes identified elsewhere as LeRoy Eltinge, then a lieutenant colonel on Pershing's staff, later a four-star general.

1. In full disclosure, as a senior in college and as a young graduate student, I developed a great relationship with Martin Blumenson, who was widowed and lived in Washington, DC, in a small apartment. For three years until the time of his death, I visited him monthly for lunch and many, many gin gimlets. In these meetings we discussed Patton often, as well as Mark Clark and other famous military figures. Most of my evolving viewpoints on Patton come not just from documents, histories, and Patton's own hand but from Martin Blumenson.

2. Patton to George S. Patton Sr., 19 April 1914, Box 6, File 1, Chronological File, January–June 1914, George S. Patton Jr. Papers, Library of Congress, Washington, DC (hereafter Patton Papers, LoC).

3. Ibid.

4. Hugh A. Drum to Patton, 6 August 1914, Box 6, File 2, Chronological File, July–December 1914, Patton Papers, LoC.

5. Patton to George S. Patton Sr., 16 May 1915, Box 6, File 4, Chronological File, April–August 1915, Patton Papers, LoC.

6. Ibid.

7. Patton to George S. Patton Sr., 12 July 1916, Box 6, File 10, Chronological File, June–October 1916, Patton Papers, LoC.

8. In the current United States Army, most officers will attain the rank of major and do so in nine to ten years. Most officers who serve thirty years or more are likely to attain the rank of colonel at a minimum.

9. Mead, *The Doughboys: America and the First World War*, 116.

10. Ibid., 117.

11. Hirshson, *General Patton: A Soldier's Life*, 116.

12. D'Este, *Patton: A Genius For War*, 273.

13. Patton to George S. Patton Sr., 12 March 1916, Box 6, File 7, Chronological File, January–March 1916, Patton Papers, LoC.

14. Ibid.

15. Patton to Captain R. F. McReynolds, 6 July 1916, Box 6, File 10, Chronological File, June–October 1916, Patton Papers, LoC.
16. See note 13.
17. Patton to George S. Patton Sr., 15 April 1916, Box 6, File 8, Chronological File, April 1916, Patton Papers, LoC.
18. Ibid.
19. Patton to George S. Patton Sr., 6 November 1917, Box 7, File 3, Chronological File, November 1917, Patton Papers, LoC.
20. See note 17.
21. Patton to Beatrice Patton, 17 May 1916, Box 6, File 9, Chronological File, May 1916, Patton Papers, LoC.
22. See note 17.
23. See note 21.
24. Patton to George S. Patton Sr., 30 April 1917, Box 6, File 14, Chronological File, February–May 1917, Patton Papers, LoC.

1. Off to Paris: Here Come the Americans

The letter quoted in the epigraph is archived in Box 6, File 16, Chronological File, July 1917, Patton Papers, LoC.

1. Mead, *The Doughboys,* 13.
2. D'Este, *Patton: A Genius for War,* 189.
3. Ibid.
4. Ibid., quoting Coffman, *The War to End All Wars,* 43.
5. The fact that the command element of the American Expeditionary Force traveled to England on a British ship was not lost on Americans and government officials at the time. Given the general unpreparedness and the necessity of speed, many soldiers of the American Expeditionary Force traveled across the Atlantic in British and French ships.
6. The modern pentathlon consists of five events, which then were shooting a pistol at 25 meters, swimming a distance of 300 meters, fencing with the dueling sword, riding a steeplechase of 5,000 meters, and running a cross-country footrace of 4,000 meters. Patton until his death believed he should have medaled in the contest, contending he did not miss a target in the pistol event but shot through a hole in the target twice. While possible, it is more than likely Patton just missed and did not want to accept it.
7. Blumenson, *The Patton Papers,* 1:391.
8. Ibid., 1:392.
9. Diary, 8 June 1917, Box 6, File 15, Chronological File, June 1917, Patton Papers, LoC.
10. Blumenson, *The Patton Papers,* 1:395.
11. Diary, 28 May 1917, Box 6, File 14, Chronological File, February–May 1917, Patton Papers, LoC.
12. Blumenson, *The Patton Papers,* 1:398.
13. Ibid., 1:426.

14. To avoid military censors, Patton seldom wrote out Pershing's name and rank and instead referred to him simply as "J" in letters home.

15. Patton to George S. Patton Sr., 15 September 1917, Box 7, File 1, Chronological File, September 1917, Patton Papers, LoC.

16. Patton to Beatrice Patton, 14 June 1917, Box 6, File 15, Chronological File, June 1917, Patton Papers, LoC.

17. Diary, 22 June 1917, Box 6, File 15, Chronological File, June 1917, Patton Papers, LoC.

18. Blumenson, *The Patton Papers*, 1:414.

19. Patton to Beatrice, 2 December 1917, Box 7, File 4, Chronological File, December 1917, Patton Papers, LoC.

20. Diary, 5 July 1917, Box 6, File 16, Chronological File, July 1917, Patton Papers, LoC.

21. Patton to Beatrice, 6 July 1917, Box 6, File 16, Chronological File, July 1917, Patton Papers, LoC.

22. Patton to Beatrice, 19 June 1917, Box 6, File 15, Chronological File, June 1917, Patton Papers, LoC.

23. Patton to Beatrice, 24 June 1917, ibid.

24. Patton to Beatrice, 25 June 1917, ibid.

25. Ibid.

26. Patton to Beatrice, 3 July 1917, Box 6, File 16, Chronological File, July 1917, Patton Papers, LoC.

27. Ibid.

28. Patton to Beatrice, 16 July 1917, ibid.

29. Patton to Beatrice, 6 July 1917, ibid.

30. Patton, undated memorandum, "Method of Getting B. to F.," Box 7, File 6, Chronological File, 13–31 December 1917, Patton Papers, LoC.

31. Patton to Beatrice, 16 August 1917, Box 6, File 17, Chronological File, August 1917, Patton Papers, LoC.

32. Patton to Beatrice, 24 August 1917, ibid.

33. Patton to Beatrice, 26 August 1917, ibid.

34. Patton to Beatrice, 29 August 1917, ibid.

35. Blumenson, *The Patton Papers*, 1:407.

36. Patton to Beatrice, 5 October 1917, Box 7, File 2, Chronological File, October 1917, Patton Papers, LoC.

37. Patton to Beatrice, 9 October 1917, ibid.

38. Patton, poem "To Beatrice," Speeches and Writings, 1900–1947, Box 74, File 1, October 1917, Patton Papers, LoC.

39. United States War Department memorandum, 15 August 1917, Box 7, File 17, Chronological File, August 1917, Patton Papers, LoC.

40. In the current United States Army Reserve, officers are generally promoted more slowly than their active-duty counterparts.

41. Patton to Beatrice, 22 September 1917, Box 7, File 1, Chronological File, September 1917, Patton Papers, LoC.

42. Patton to Beatrice, 2 September 1917, ibid.

43. Patton to Beatrice, 22 August 1917, Box 6, File 17, Chronological File, August 1917, Patton Papers, LoC.

44. D'Este, *Patton: A Genius for War,* 197, quoting Vandiver, *Black Jack,* 2:743–44.

45. Blumenson, *Patton: The Man behind the Legend,* 95.

46. Blumenson, *The Patton Papers,* 1:403.

47. Hirshson, *General Patton: A Soldier's Life,* 98.

48. Patton to Beatrice, 19 September 1917, Box 7, File 1, Chronological File, September 1917, Patton Papers, LoC.

49. Patton to Beatrice, 2 September 1917, ibid.

50. Patton to Beatrice, 19 September 1917, ibid.

51. Patton to Beatrice, 30 September 1917, ibid.

52. Patton to Beatrice, 9 October 1917, Box 7, File 2, Chronological File, October 1917, Patton Papers, LoC.

53. Diary, 30 September 1917, Box 7, File 1, Chronological File, September 1917, Patton Papers, LoC.

54. Patton to General John J. Pershing, 3 October 1917, Box 25, File 6, Correspondence, 1903–1945, Patton Papers, LoC.

55. Patton to Beatrice, 24 October 1917, Box 7, File 2, Chronological File, October 1917, Patton Papers, LoC.

56. Diary, 3 November 1917, Box 7, File 3, Chronological File, October 1917, Patton Papers, LoC.

57. Ibid.

58. Patton to George S. Patton Sr., 6 November 1917, Box 7, File 3, Chronological File, November 1917, Patton Papers, LoC.

59. Diary, 5 December 1917, Box 7, File 6, Chronological File, 13–31 December 1917, Patton Papers, LoC.

2. Land Crabs, Land Ironclads, Landships: The Tank

The letter quoted in the epigraph is archived in Box 7, File 2, Chronological File, October 1917, Patton Papers, LoC.

1. Wright, *Tank,* 23.

2. Ibid., 24.

3. D'Este, *Patton: A Genius for War,* 202.

4. Farago, *Patton: Ordeal and Triumph,* 72.

5. Ibid.

6. Ibid.

7. Wright, *Tank,* 29.

8. Ibid.

9. For a picture of the Mark I, see Fitzsimons, *Tanks and Weapons of World War I.*

10. The three French tanks are pictured in the same volume.

11. Fitzsimons, *Tanks and Weapons of World War I,* 99.

12. Ibid., 98.

13. Wilson, *Treat 'em Rough!,* 4.

14. A "female" tank was a tank that had only a machine gun and no cannon. A "male" tank was one that had only a cannon.

15. Wright, *Tank,* 49.

16. Ibid.

17. D'Este, *Patton: A Genius for War,* 202.

18. Ibid., 203.

19. Sources vary on the number of tanks used in the attack; 378 is the number used in current research and study.

20. Wren, *The Great Battles of World War I,* 316.

21. Wright, *Tank,* 77.

22. Ibid., 79.

23. Patton to Beatrice Patton, 26 November 1917, Box 7, File 3, Chronological File, November 1917, Patton Papers, LoC.

24. Patton to Beatrice, 9 November 1917, ibid.

25. Patton, "Memorandum on Military Appearance and Saluting," 12 November 1917, ibid.

26. Diary, 19 November 1917, ibid.

27. Patton to Beatrice, 20 November 1917, ibid.

28. Patton, United States Tank Corps report, 11–12 December 1917, Box 7, File 5, Chronological File, 11–12 December 1917, Patton Papers, LoC.

29. Blumenson, *The Patton Papers,* 1:437.

30. Hirshson, *General Patton: A Soldier's Life,* 103.

31. Blumenson, *The Patton Papers,* 1:437.

32. Hirshson, *General Patton: A Soldier's Life,* 103.

33. Farago, *Patton: Ordeal and Triumph,* 77.

34. Blumenson, *The Patton Papers,* 1:438.

35. Ibid.

36. Farago, *Patton: Ordeal and Triumph,* 74.

37. United States Army, Center of Military History, *United States Army in World War I, 1917–1919,* 8:15.

38. D'Este, *Patton: A Genius for War,* 211.

39. An interesting side note: While Patton commanded and trained tankers in France, a then unknown, newly promoted lieutenant colonel by the name of Dwight D. Eisenhower commanded and trained tankers at Camp Colt, Pennsylvania. Following the war, the two would become best friends and constantly discuss tanks and tactics with one another. Sadly, their relationship grew distant and eventually deteriorated during World War II, and the two never made up before Patton's death. Martin Blumenson blamed Eisenhower more than Patton for the breakdown in their once very close friendship.

40. Blumenson, *Patton: The Man behind the Legend,* 102.

41. Patton to Beatrice, 14 December 1917, Box 7, File 6, Chronological File, 13–31 December 1917, Patton Papers, LoC.

42. Col. H. W. Brewster, memorandum for Chief of Staff, 19 July 1917, Box 1, File 8, Correspondence and Memoranda 1889–1945, 1917, Samuel Rockenbach Papers, Virginia Military Institute, Lexington, VA (hereafter Rockenbach Papers, VMI).

43. Memorandum from Adjutant General American Expeditionary Force Headquarters, 18 January 1918, Box 1, File 9, Correspondence and Memoranda 1889–1945, January–June 1918, Rockenbach Papers, VMI.

44. Inter-Allied Tank Committee minutes, 6–7 May 1918, Box 3, File 4, Inter-Allied Tank Committee Session 1, 1918, 6–7 May, Rockenbach Papers, VMI.

45. Ibid., 3.

46. Patton memo, 2 May 1918, Box 3, File 9, Inter-Allied Tank Committee Related Docs—Reports by Patton, 1918, Rockenbach Papers, VMI.

47. Inter-Allied Tank Committee minutes, 6–7 May 1918 (see note 44), 20.

48. Ibid.

49. Ibid., 7.

50. Ibid., 9.

51. Inter-Allied Tank Committee minutes, 8 July 1918, Box 3, File 7, Inter-Allied Tank Committee Session 3, 1918, July 1918, Rockenbach Papers, VMI.

52. Inter-Allied Tank Committee minutes, 6–7 May 1918 (see note 44), 10.

53. Reports and Resolutions, 6–7 May 1918, Box 3, File 5, Inter-Allied Tank Committee Session 1, 1918, 6–7 May, Rockenbach Papers, VMI.

54. Inter-Allied Tank Committee minutes, 8 July 1918 (see note 51), 8.

55. Ibid.

56. See note 46.

57. Patton, United States Tank Corps report, 11–12 December 1917, Box 7, File 5, Chronological File, 11–12 December 1917, Patton Papers, LoC.

58. Ibid., 1.

59. Ibid.

60. Ibid., 14.

61. Ibid., 15.

62. Ibid., 16.

63. Ibid., 17.

64. Blumenson, *The Patton Papers,* 1:454–55.

65. Patton, United States Tank Corps report, 11–12 December 1917 (see note 57), section C.

66. Ibid.

67. Ibid.

68. Ibid., section D.

69. Ibid.

70. Ibid.

71. Ibid.

72. Ibid.

73. Patton to Beatrice, 14 December 1917, Box 7, File 6, Chronological File, 13–31 December 1918, Patton Papers, LoC.

74. Patton to Beatrice, 23 December 1917, ibid.

3. The Tank Master: Patton and the Tank Center

The letter quoted in the epigraph is archived in Box 7, File 7, Chronological File, 1–20 January 1918, Patton Papers, LoC.

1. Blumenson, *The Patton Papers*, 456.
2. The United States Heavy Tank School was located in Wool, Dorset, England.
3. Patton to Beatrice Patton, 14 January 1918, Box 7, File 7, Chronological File, 1–20 January 1918, Patton Papers, LoC.
4. Patton to Beatrice, 23 January 1918, Box 7, File 8, Chronological File, 21–31 January 1918, Patton Papers, LoC.
5. Ibid.
6. Patton to Beatrice, 25 January 1918, Box 7, File 8, Chronological File, 21–31 January 1918, Patton Papers, LoC.
7. Blumenson, *The Patton Papers*, 1:478.
8. Ibid.
9. See note 3.
10. Patton to Beatrice, 27 January 1918, Box 7, File 8, Chronological File, 21–31 January 1918, Patton Papers, LoC.
11. Diary, 31 January 1918, ibid.
12. Patton to Beatrice, 30 January 1918, ibid.
13. See note 3.
14. Diary, 1 February 1918, Box 7, File 9, Chronological File, 1–10 February 1918, Patton Papers, LoC.
15. Patton to Beatrice, 8 February 1918, ibid.
16. Patton, memorandum for the Adjutant, 23 February 1918, Box 7, File 11, Chronological File, 18–28 February 1918, Patton Papers, LoC.
17. Hirshson, *General Patton: A Soldier's Life*, 114.
18. Ibid.
19. Patton, "Lecture on Discipline to 304th Tank Brigade," 18 March 1918, Box 67, File 1, Speeches and Writings, February–July 1918, Patton Papers, LoC.
20. Blumenson, *The Patton Papers*, 1:493.
21. Patton to Beatrice, 17 February 1918, Box 7, File 10, Chronological File, 11–17 February 1918, Patton Papers, LoC.
22. Patton to Beatrice, 27 February 1918, Box 7, File 11, Chronological File, 18–28 February 1918, Patton Papers, LoC.
23. Blumenson, *The Patton Papers*, 1:497.
24. Patton to Beatrice, 19 March 1918, Box 7, File 12, Chronological File, 1–24 March 1918, Patton Papers, LoC.
25. Diary, 21 March 1918, ibid.
26. Patton to Beatrice, 22 March 1918, ibid.
27. Patton to Beatrice, 24 March 1918, ibid.
28. Blumenson, *The Patton Papers*, 1:509.
29. Patton to Ellie Ayer, 28 March 1918, Box 7, File 13, Chronological File, 25–31 March 1918, Patton Papers, LoC.
30. Patton, undated memorandum, March 1918, Box 7, File 13, Chronological File, 25–31 March 1918, Patton Papers, LoC.
31. Patton to Beatrice, 10 April 1918, Box 8, File 1, Chronological File, 1–10 April 1918, Patton Papers, LoC.
32. The Pattons would welcome their third child and only son, George S. Patton IV, on Christmas Eve in 1923.

132 Notes to Pages 55–64

33. Patton to Beatrice, 22 April 1918, Box 8, File 3, Chronological File, 18–30 April 1918, Patton Papers, LoC.

34. Blumenson, *The Patton Papers*, 1:525.

35. Ibid., 1:531.

36. Ibid., 1:533.

37. Patton to Beatrice, 30 May 1918, Box 8, File 6, Chronological File, 26–31 May 1918, Patton Papers, LoC.

38. Ibid.

39. Patton to Beatrice, 3 June 1918, Box 8, File 7, Chronological File, 1–7 June 1918, Patton Papers, LoC.

40. Blumenson, *The Patton Papers*, 1:539.

41. Diary, 6 June 1918, Box 8, File 7, Chronological File, 1–7 June 1918, Patton Papers, LoC.

42. "History of the 304th (1st) Tank Brigade United States Tank Corps," 1918, Box 67, File 4, Speeches and Writings, 1918–1920, Patton Papers, LoC, 6.

43. To avoid confusion, the original number designations will be used until they are changed before the Meuse-Argonne offensive.

44. Blumenson, *The Patton Papers*, 1:540.

45. Hirshson, *General Patton: A Soldier's Life*, 120.

46. Patton, lecture to General Staff College, 22 July 1918, Box 8, File 9, Chronological File, July 1918, Patton Papers, LoC, 1.

47. Ibid., 5.

48. See note 15.

49. Patton, lecture to General Staff College (see note 46), 5.

50. Patton to Beatrice, 18 July 1918, Box 8, File 9, Chronological File, July 1918, Patton Papers, LoC.

51. George S. Patton Sr. to Patton, 20 February 1919, Box 9, File 11, Chronological File, 11–28 February 1919, Patton Papers, LoC.

52. Lieutenant Colonel D. D. Pullen to Patton, 5 July 1918, Box 8, File 9, Chronological File, July 1918, Patton Papers, LoC.

53. "History of the 304th (1st) Tank Brigade" (see note 42), 10.

4. Combat: St. Mihiel

The letter quoted in the epigraph is archived in Box 8, File 15, Chronological File, 13–16 September 1918, Patton Papers, LoC.

1. D'Este, *Patton: A Genius for War*, 236, has a helpful map.

2. Mead, *The Doughboys*, 285.

3. D'Este, *Patton: A Genius for War*, 230.

4. An American division in World War I was incredibly large, consisting of around 29,000 men, almost double the size of French and British divisions.

5. Fuller, *Decisive Battles of the U.S.A.*, 380.

6. Blumenson, *The Patton Papers*, 1:368.

7. Patton to George S. Patton Sr., 20 August 1918, Box 8, File 10, Chronological File, 1–20 August 1918, Patton Papers, LoC.

8. Patton to Beatrice, 28 August 1918, Box 8, File 11, Chronological File, 21–28 August 1918, Patton Papers, LoC.

9. Blumenson, *The Patton Papers,* 1:575.

10. Blumenson, *Patton: The Man behind the Legend,* 107.

11. "History of the 304th (1st) Tank Brigade United States Tank Corps," 1918, Box 67, File 4, Speeches and Writings, 1918–1920, Patton Papers, LoC, 10.

12. Ibid., 12.

13. Ibid.

14. Ibid., 13.

15. Patton, "First Tank Brigade Field Order No. 1," 9 September 1918, Box 8, File 14, Chronological File, 9–12 September 1918, Patton Papers, LoC, 1.

16. Ibid., 2.

17. Ibid., 3.

18. Ibid., 4.

19. Blumenson, *Patton: The Man behind the Legend,* 107.

20. Patton to Beatrice, 16 September 1918, Box 8, File 15, Chronological File, 13–16 September 1918, Patton Papers, LoC.

21. Blumenson, *The Patton Papers,* 1:578.

22. Blumenson, *The Patton Papers,* 1;582.

23. Mead, *The Doughboys,* 285.

24. See note 20.

25. Ibid.

26. Patton to George S. Patton Sr., 20 September 1918, Box 8, File 16, Chronological File, 17–30 September 1918, Patton Papers, LoC.

27. Blumenson, *The Patton Papers,* 1:585.

28. See note 20.

29. Hirshson, *General Patton: A Soldier's Life,* 126.

30. "History of the 304th (1st) Tank Brigade" (see note 11), 18.

31. Ibid.

32. Ibid.

33. See note 20.

34. Ibid.

35. Ibid.

36. Patton and Compton, *War Diary 1918,* 12.

37. Mead, *The Doughboys,* 297.

38. Patton to Beatrice, 19 September 1918, Box 8, File 16, Chronological File, 17–30 September 1918, Patton Papers, LoC.

39. "History of the 304th (1st) Tank Brigade" (see note 11), 16.

40. Ibid.

41. Ibid.

42. Ibid., 17.

43. Ibid.

44. Ibid., 18.

45. Ibid., 19.

46. Ibid.

47. Ibid.

48. Ibid.

49. Operations report, 304th Tank Brigade United States Corps, 12–15 September 1918, Box 8, File 15, Chronological File, 13–16 September 1918, Patton Papers, LoC.

50. See note 20.

51. Blumenson, *The Patton Papers,* 1:597.

52. Hirshson, *General Patton: A Soldier's Life,* 127.

53. General John J. Pershing to Brigadier General Samuel Rockenbach, 16 September 1918, Box 8, File 15, Chronological File, 13–16 September 1918, Patton Papers, LoC.

54. Rockenbach to Pershing, 16 September 1918, ibid.

55. Mead, *The Doughboys,* 299.

56. Hirshson, *General Patton: A Soldier's Life,* 128.

5. The True Test: The Meuse-Argonne Offensive

The letter quoted in the epigraph is archived in Box 9, File 1, Chronological File, 19–29 October 1918, Patton Papers, LoC.

1. "History of the 304th (1st) Tank Brigade United States Tank Corps," 1918, Box 67, File 4, Speeches and Writings, 1918–1920, Patton Papers, LoC, 28.

2. Ibid., 29.

3. Ibid., 30.

4. Blumenson, *The Patton Papers,* 1:609.

5. Patton to Beatrice, 26 September 1918, Box 8, File 16, Chronological File, 17–30 September 1918, Patton Papers, LoC.

6. Ibid.

7. Diary, 26 September 1918, ibid.

8. "History of the 304th (1st) Tank Brigade" (see note 1), 31.

9. Ibid.

10. Patton to Beatrice, 28 September 1918, Box 8, File 16, Chronological File, 17–30 September 1918, Patton Papers, LoC.

11. "History of the 304th (1st) Tank Brigade" (see note 1), 32.

12. See note 10.

13. Mikolashek, "The Slapping Incident: The Public Reaction," 3.

14. Sworn statement by First Lieutenant Paul S. Edwards, 27 November 1918, Box 9, File 4, Chronological File, 21–30 November 1918, Patton Papers, LoC.

15. See note 10.

16. See note 14.

17. Blumenson, *The Patton Papers,* 1:613.

18. See note 14.

19. Sworn Statement by Private First Class Joseph Angelo, 21 November 1918, Box 9, File 4, Chronological File, 21–30 November 1918, Patton Papers, LoC.

20. Blumenson, *The Patton Papers,* 1:615.

21. Ibid., 1:621.
22. See note 10.
23. Blumenson, *Patton: The Man behind the Legend*, 114.
24. "History of the 304th (1st) Tank Brigade" (see note 1), 33.
25. Ibid., 34.
26. Ibid.
27. Ibid., 35.
28. Ibid., 36.
29. Ibid.
30. Ibid., 39.
31. Ibid.
32. Ibid., 41.
33. Ibid.
34. Ibid., 43.
35. Ibid.
36. Fuller, *Decisive Battles of the U.S.A.*, 394.
37. "History of the 304th (1st) Tank Brigade" (see note 1), 45.
38. Ibid., 47.
39. Ibid., 70.
40. Ibid., 71.
41. Ibid., 72.
42. Patton to Major Sereno Brett, 25 November 1918, Box 67, File 4, Speeches and Writings, November–December 1918, Patton Papers, LoC.
43. The source of the observations in this section is "Tanks from the German Point of View," n.d., Box 55, File 2, Tanks: Reports: General, 1918–1919, Patton Papers, LoC.

6. The Spoils of War: Rest, Recovery, and Peace

The letter quoted in the epigraph is archived in Box 9, File 1, Chronological File, 19–29 October 1918, Patton Papers, LoC.

1. Patton to Beatrice, 2 October 1918, Box 9, File 1, Chronological File, 1–18 October 1918, Patton Papers, LoC.
2. Patton to Beatrice, 4 October 1918, ibid.
3. Ibid.
4. Thomas M. Johnson, "Col. Patten, Hero of the Tanks," *Evening Sun* clipping, n.d. [October 1918].
5. Patton to Beatrice, 10 October 1918, Box 9, File 1, Chronological File, 1–18 October 1918, Patton Papers, LoC.
6. Ibid.
7. Patton to Beatrice, 15 October 1918, ibid.
8. American Expeditionary Force Headquarters Special Orders Number 290, 10 October 1918, Box 9, File 1, Chronological File, 1–18 October 1918, Patton Papers, LoC.
9. Patton to Beatrice, 17 October 1918, ibid.

10. Ibid.

11. Patton to Beatrice, 26 October 1918, Box 9, File 2, Chronological File, 19–29 October 1918, Patton Papers, LoC.

12. Patton to Beatrice, 20 October 1918, ibid.

13. 302nd Tank Center General Order Number 2, 29 October 1918, ibid.

14. Diary, 11 November 1918, Box 9, File 3, Chronological File, 3–20 November 1918, Patton Papers, LoC.

15. Patton, "In Memory of Captain English, Tank Corps," 11 November 1918, Box 3, File 10A, Subject File Patton, Rockenbach Papers, VMI.

16. Patton to Beatrice, 16 November 1918, Box 9, File 3, Chronological File, 3–20 November 1918, Patton Papers, LoC.

17. Blumenson, *The Patton Papers,* 1:622.

18. See note 9.

19. Patton to Beatrice, 18 November 1918, Box 9, File 3, Chronological File, 3–20 November 1918, Patton Papers, LoC.

20. Ibid.

21. Blumenson, *The Patton Paper,* 645.

22. Diary, 29 November 1918, Box 9, File 4, Chronological File, 21–30 November 1918, Patton Papers, LoC.

23. Patton, "Lecture on Tank Tactics," 20 November 1918, Box 9, File 3, Chronological File, 3–20 November 1918, Patton Papers, LoC.

24. Operations report, 304th Tank Brigade United States Corps, 18 November 1918, ibid.

25. Diary, 4 December 1918, Box 9, File 6, Chronological File, 4–22 December 1918, Patton Papers, LoC.

26. United States War Department General Orders Number 133, 16 December 1918, ibid.

27. Patton to Beatrice, 11 December 1918, ibid.

28. Beatrice to Patton, 16 December 1918, ibid.

29. Patton to George S. Patton Sr., 8 January 1919, Box 9, File 8, Chronological File, 1–10 January 1919, Patton Papers, LoC.

30. Patton to Beatrice, 7 February 1919, Box 9, File 10, Chronological File, 1–20 February 1919, Patton Papers, LoC.

31. Patton to Beatrice, 10 February 1919, ibid.

32. Blumenson, *The Patton Papers,* 1:687.

33. Ibid., 1:695.

7. The War after the War: The Fight for the United States Tank Corps

The letter quoted in the epigraph is archived in Box 9, File 13, Chronological File, April–August 1919, Patton Papers, LoC.

1. Patton to George S. Patton Sr., 1 April 1919, Box 9, File 13, Chronological File, April–August 1919, Patton Papers, LoC.

2. Patton to Brigadier General Samuel Rockenbach, 24 February 1918, Box 3, File 10A, Subject File Patton, Rockenbach Papers, VMI.

3. Rockenbach to Beatrice Patton, 23 February 1945, ibid.

4. Ibid.

5. United States Tank Corps Headquarters Special Order Number 63, 22 April 1919, Box 9, File 13, Chronological File, April–August 1919, Patton Papers, LoC.

6. D'Este, *Patton: A Genius for War,* 288.

7. Ibid., 287.

8. Patton to Rockenbach, 27 March 1919, Box 3, File 10A, Subject File Patton, Rockenbach Papers, VMI.

9. Patton to Rockenbach, 4 August 1919, ibid.

10. United States Army Injury Medical Form, 22 January 1920, Box 9, File 16, Chronological File, January–April 1920, Patton Papers, LoC.

11. Patton, *Cavalry and Tanks in Future Wars,* 24.

12. Ibid., 24–25.

13. Ibid., 25.

14. Ibid., 31.

15. Ibid., 35.

16. Ibid., 36.

Conclusion

1. Patton to Beatrice, 19 October 1918, Box 9, File 2, Chronological File, 19–29 October 1918, Patton Papers, LoC.

2. Wilson, *Treat 'em Rough!,* vi.

Selected Bibliography

Primary Sources

Blumenson, Martin, ed. *The Patton Papers*. Vol. 1, *1885–1940*. Boston: Houghton Mifflin, 1972.

National Archives II, Special Media Archives Services Division, College Park, MD. Record Group 111.

Patton, George S. *Cavalry and Tanks in Future Wars*. Edited by Aleksandra M. Rohde. Alexandria, VA: Dale Street, 2017.

————. Papers. Manuscript Division, Library of Congress, Washington, DC.

————. *See also* Blumenson, *The Patton Papers*.

Patton, George S., Jr., and Ranulf Compton. *War Diary 1918*. Edited by Aleksandra M. Rohde. Alexandria, VA: Dale Street, 2018.

Rockenbach, Samuel. Papers. Virginia Military Institute, Lexington, VA.

United States Army, Center of Military History. *United States Army in World War I, 1917–1919*. Vol. 8. Washington, DC: US Government Press, 1990.

Secondary Sources

Blumenson, Martin. *Patton: The Man behind the Legend, 1885–1945*. New York: William Morrow, 1985.

Coffman, Edward M. *The War to End All Wars*. New York: Oxford University Press, 1968.

D'Este, Carlo. *Patton: A Genius for War*. 1995. New York: Harper Perennial, 1997.

Farago, Ladislas. *Patton: Ordeal and Triumph*. New York: Dell, 1963.

Fitzsimons, Bernard. *Tanks and Weapons of World War I*. Turnhout: BPC, 1973.

Fuller, J. F. C. *Decisive Battles of the U.S.A.* New York: Thomas Yoseloff, 1942.

Hirshson, Stanley P. *General Patton: A Soldier's Life*. New York: HarperCollins, 2002.

Mead, Gary. *The Doughboys: America and the First World War*. New York: Overlook Press, 2000.

Mikolashek, Jon. "The Slapping Incident: The Public Reaction." George C. Marshall Scholar Program paper, 2002.

Vandiver, Frank E. *Black Jack: The Life and Times of John J. Pershing.* College Station: Texas A&M University Press, 1977.

Wilson, Dale E. *Treat 'em Rough! The Birth of American Armor, 1917–20.* Novato, CA: Presidio Press, 1990.

Wren, Jack. *The Great Battles of World War I.* New York: Grosset & Dunlap/ Madison Square Press, 1971.

Wright, Patrick. *Tank.* New York: Viking, 2002.

Index